A Man and His Convictions

Jay Wegter

FOREWORD

A Man and His Convictions

The Workbook is much more than a book on men's sexual purity. Our aim is to focus on the connection between sexual purity and biblical masculinity. Godly manhood is inseparable from the imperative to keep growing toward spiritual maturity commanded in Scripture.

The chapters in the Workbook are organized in such a way that spiritual growth is the goal. We refer to this pathway toward growth and completeness in Christ as the "maturity map." The Workbook is 'mapped out' into three parts or aspects of godly manhood. A man's convictions shape his character which shapes his ministry: Book one, CONVICTION > which leads to Book two, CHARACTER > which leads to Book three, COMPETENCY in our CALLING. Each of the chapters in these three sections provides essential content for progress in biblical discipleship. Thus, in using the Workbook, the mentor or Bible study leader can be deliberate in moving his disciple through stages of growth.

The Workbook gives Christian men the vital tools necessary to construct a strategy for sexual purity. It is paramount that we are utterly intentional and strategic at this point. Here is the reason why: for most men sexual lust is the greatest obstacle standing in the way of their growth in holiness, undivided devotion to Christ, and preparation for service in the body of Christ.

Without preaching in a moralistic manner, the Workbook reveals how porn harms its users and those in relationship with them. You'll learn why the use of internet porn deepens selfishness. By contrast, Scripture commands us to have our senses trained in righteousness (Heb 5:14) rather than a heart trained in lust and greed (2 Pet 2:14). Through habitual porn use new deadly pathways are 'welded' or formed in the nervous system—this one of the reasons why porn is so addictive. In addition, its false offer of fulfillment is one of the greatest mirages or illusions imaginable. When a man brings his desires to porn, it is like filling one's mouth with hot sand and gravel in order to satisfy your thirst. Porn sows to our yearning for intimacy, gives a brief moment of excitement and pleasure; but has no hope of producing oneness with another person.

Porn use signals a crisis in a man's masculinity. Praise God there is deliverance in Christ. In the Workbook you'll see that the answer is to this pervasive problem is a redeemed sexuality in Christ. Redeemed sexuality results in unhindered growth in true masculinity.

Godly masculinity, discipleship, spiritual maturity, and servant leadership all operate together. Therefore, winning sexual freedom in Christ is tied to progress in each of these areas of godly manhood. Victory is the mandate if a man is to fulfill his calling to lead, guide, instruct, protect, provide, serve, love, cherish, risk, initiate, give self, communicate, and model holiness. These character qualities require that a man have sexual freedom in Christ, and not be in bondage to lust. The Workbook explains the 'how to'.

As we planned this book, our alternate subtitle was, "Understanding the Devil's Playbook—what it takes to win Sexual Freedom in Christ." We did shorten it but want the reader to understand that every square inch of victory in our sexual freedom involves skill and spiritual warfare. Rather than a book narrowly focused on abstinence, or overcoming sexual lust, our Workbook integrates the positives of Christian worldview, gospel-centered sanctification, biblical discipleship, and godly masculinity.

The Workbook is intensely realistic in facing the challenges of living in a culture which worships sex. Sexual lust, porn and immorality are idols which compete with a believer's determination to follow Christ. Christians need a well thought out strategy for personal holiness—that is a central purpose of the

Workbook. Our affections inform our priorities—which is why the Christian must build a perimeter around the heart. A desire unworthy of Christ (an idol) can only be replaced and removed by deepening our love and adoration of Christ, our true treasure.

Another important element in the strategy you will learn is how to 'out-truth' the lie. Like an elite soldier who is member of a SEAL team, consider yourself on a 'search and destroy mission'. Your task is to search out lies and destroy them with the truth of God's Word. The Christian is on a mission to eliminate every lie that offers itself to us—'taking every thought captive to the obedience of Christ'.

In the Workbook, you'll be introduced to new concepts which will help you recognize and overcome the most pervasive lies in our culture (lies such as the 'Gnostic disconnect'). Porn finds one of is most common entry gates in the false disconnect between soul and body. Body and soul are created by God to operate as a unit—they work together expressing our loyalties and exhibiting who our true master is. Scripture keep body and spirit joined; thus the true nature of spirituality is that the body is a temple and living sacrifice unto the Lord. But in the Gnostic disconnect lie, the body and spirit are not viewed as unified, or operating together, but are considered separate domains. This lie creates the problem of a divided life which divorces the spiritual from the physical. So, rather than informing one another in unified action, the body is treated as physical 'shell' only instead of the center of human will. This opens the door to sexual immorality.

Another closely related lie today is that the human body (and our sexuality) is but a blank canvas upon which we may write our own identity and desires. God's Word says the opposite. Our bodies are 'for the Lord' (1 Cor 6:13). Porn is a lying worldview about the body and its purpose. God's goal, design, and blueprint for the use of our bodies is intended for His glory and our good. Our bodies are the greatest spiritual resource we have by which we serve God by serving the brethren. God's plan and design for the creation (including our bodies) falls under a category of thought known as cosmology. Your body is part of

God's design for His creation, and how you use of your body reveals your world and life view, and your spirituality.

The Workbook is intended to overcome a common misconception in the church today: that a man can be changed morally and spiritually in the sight of God apart from the cross and the gospel. The message of new life in Christ answers the questions: how can we change, where does the ability come from to be more like Christ? What is necessary to obey the transformation mandate set forth in God's Word? In terms of the source of power and enablement, the law of God can't do it. The power to change is found in the gospel of the cross of Christ. God's way is not to improve the sinner, for the cross 'bankrupts us' until we abandon self-reliance. Yet in the cross we find our resources for holiness. All motives for good works come from the cross. In the glorious good news of the gospel believers are righteousness by faith—through faith in Christ they have a 'God-approved' righteousness without works which actually prepares the way for good works. Now it is Christ's works through the believer (Gal 2:20).

You will find your heart enlarging to take in more of the majesty of our Lord as you enjoy the chapters on the manhood of Christ and God's 'glory story' in Christ. Most of all, the Workbook is written in a style to encourage the growing believer so that he or she finds their all in all in God's provision of our Great and Merciful High Priest.

TABLE OF CONTENTS

ACKNOWLEDGEMENTS

It goes without saying that the work of our merciful Savior in my own life is the only reason this book could be written. The Lord in His unfailing love has been relentless in His determination to make me into a godly man through the work of Christ. Years of self-serving narcissism logged during 'the reproach of my youth' had to be methodically replaced with biblical thinking and acting. In many ways, the sequence of our Workbooks: *Conviction > Character > Calling* is very much autobiographical. For it is my own testimony of spiritual progress by the transforming power of God's truth in the inner man through the power of the Spirit.

I would like to express my deep appreciation for the assistance of the brethren on this project. Gratitude is due to the Christian friends who have served as selfless volunteers, sacrificially giving of their time and dedication. Much appreciation goes to our editors: Kevin Bell, Stephen Duwe, and Paul Kern. Their ability to see the text 'through the eyes of the reader' was invaluable. In terms of excellence, their editing changes have helped make the difference when portions of the book needed clarification and illustration. Also many thanks go to my young friend Zach Beggs who has become an invaluable ministry partner from the 'millennial' generation. Zach's boundless energy, creativity and post-production skills have brought this project squarely into the 21st Century. Our entire Gospel for Life team is anticipating how Zach's efforts in graphics and production will broaden the reach of this ministry, giving us an entirely new venue with E-book exposure to new audiences. May all the glory go to our God and Savior; for our prayer is that His truth communicated and applied in this book will be a tool for building up the saints unto a mature man (Eph 4:13).

The sting of death is sin, and the power of sin is the law; but thanks be to God, who gives us the victory through our Lord Jesus Christ. Therefore, my beloved brethren, be steadfast, immovable, always abounding in the work of the Lord, knowing that your toil is not *in* vain in the Lord (1 Cor 15:56-58).

A Ministry of

Gospel For Life,
www.gospelforlife.org

Jay Wegter

Section 1
Biblical Cosmology

Section Objectives

1. Understanding creation and purpose; biblical cosmology and God's plan for sexual oneness.

2. The act of private lust is a selfish act independent from God.

3. Those who refuse to repent *are living on borrowed time Romans 2:5-9.*

4. The problem and consequence of a divided life.

5. Through the cross, finding our deliverance from the rule of sin.

Creation & Purpose

Every aspect of creation was made for a purpose. Cosmology (the biblical study of the nature of the universe) shows us how all things are unified by God's design for His creation. Mankind in God's plan is the most significant part of the universe (Ps 8). Teleology (God's perfect goal of creation) tells us the purpose of our sexuality and how it fits in His plan. We will apply these two concepts of cosmology and teleology to give us **the divine perspective of sexuality**. My hope is that you will place a higher value on God's gift of marital oneness. Since God created us as sexual beings, we need to return to biblical cosmology in order to better understand God's intentions for the gift of sexual oneness. Rather than merely asking what we should or should not do (or what is permissible), we ought to ask why did God create sex and **how does He intend that our sexuality bring glory to Himself?**

The purpose of this chapter is to help us more fully see all of life from the vantage point of biblical cosmology. It is absolutely essential that we do so if we are to be discerning and if we are to avoid the snares in our culture which are taking souls captive (Col 2:8).

---

*[8] See to it that no one takes you captive by philosophy and empty deceit, according to human tradition, according to the elemental spirits of the world, and **not according** to Christ. Colossians 2:8 ESV*

When we view our entire existence from the perspective of biblical cosmology it is intensely satisfying because it shows us how all things are unified by God's design and brought into their proper relations.

Watch the biblical cosmology introduction on the bundled DVD by Professor Jay Wegter

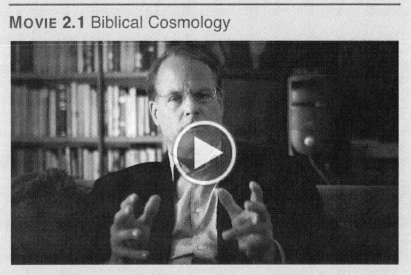

MOVIE **2.1** Biblical Cosmology

Listen to **Movie 2.1** as professor Jay Wegter introduces the chapter on biblical cosmology and the effect on our creation and purpose.

Our culture is sending a radically different message: **secular humanism and postmodernism suggest that we have the power** to order our own little universes and make our own rules. This is man making up his own cosmology—and dismissing God's design as if it is inconsequential (without consequence).

The Word of God corrects this willful ignorance of our age by constantly reminding us that created reality is a perfect co-mingling of creational and moral order (Ps 96). This deficiency in understanding is commonly expressed as, "Sure we will let God be Lord of the Christian religion; but we will not bow to His claims to be Lord of history, Lord of the cosmos, and Lord of our bodies." How reminiscent this attitude is of the second Psalm, *"Let us tear their fetters apart, and cast away their cords from us!"*

Cosmology begins with the fact that God made all things out of nothing. He is Creator, Upholder, and Definer of what He has made. This has profound ethical ramifications for our lives. For if we define something other than the way God does, or if we use something in a way God forbids, **we are engaging in direct revolt** against His Person. We must understand through our study of cosmology that God is ultimate owner and ruler over all, and we His creatures are stewards and co-rulers over His creation (Ps 8). Since man was created to be both a steward of the physical and moral order, we are not owners. As stewards we will give an account of our stewardship (Rom 14:11-12).

---

[11]As I live, says the Lord, every knee shall bow to me, and every tongue shall confess to God." *[12]So then each of us will give an account of himself to God. Romans 14:11-12 ESV*

Have we used what was entrusted to us for the purpose of serving and honoring God? To take the blessings of God for self without a view to be a faithful steward is to be a usurper. Lucifer was the first usurper.

The Private Issue of Lust vs. Purity

In an act of covetousness and theft, the devil sought to take for himself what was not his that he might use it for selfish purposes. All who are followers of Satan are engaged in the **same covetous acts of usurpation**. Human usurpers **refuse to pay the modest 'rent'** of a lifestyle of thanksgiving unto God—as a consequence, like their spiritual father, the devil, they are engaged in the **theft of God's rightful glory and honor.** Romans 2 makes it abundantly clear that **usurpers are living on borrowed time** (Rom 2:5-9).

5But because of your hard and impenitent heart you are storing up wrath for yourself on the day of wrath when God's righteous judgment will be revealed. 6He will render to each one according to his works: 7 to those who by patience in well-doing seek for glory and honor and immortality, he will give eternal life; 8 but for those who are self-seeking and do not obey the truth, but obey unrighteousness, there will be wrath and fury. 9 There will be tribulation and distress for every human being who does evil, the Jew first and also the Greek. Romans 2:5-9 ESV

Biblical cosmology immediately impacts the issue of our battle for purity as Christian men and women. The hypnotic draw of illicit images is in part tied to an anatomical ideal for the fairer sex. When yanked from this divinely ordained context, anatomical beauty is an idol; **(the worship of the creature instead of the Creator) involves tearing portions of God's creation from their 'habitat' as creation structures and selfishly using them for our lusts instead of for God's glory.** Pornography has the destructive power to fragment our acting and thinking because it **advances the deception that human anatomy can stand apart from God's 'glory purposes'.**

We know that the craving for sexual intimacy tends to be a driving force in men—frequently tempting us to set aside God's cosmology (His plan for man and woman). But, to indulge in illicit erotic images instead of pursuing sexual oneness within the marriage bond is ultimately unsatisfying. Smut leaves one empty, hollow, and distant from God. The false promise of satisfaction proves to be a mirage.

Sexual Oneness & Cosmology

Cosmology tells us why this is the case. Sexual oneness was created to consummate and build the covenant bond of marital oneness to the glory of God. Therefore, to use sexual stimulation **NOT** for the purpose of marital oneness but for self-gratification represents a rejection of God's design and a covetous usurpation of God's good gift—using it for selfish purposes. No wonder guilt, shame, and self-hate follow sexual impurity. For those who do not repent (refusing to radically change directions), God's judgment will one day hit like a sledgehammer.

Now here is where biblical cosmology can be a mighty weapon in our arsenal against the bondage of sexual lust. Our culture offers us the lie of a divided life—as if we can successfully live with a set of beliefs which contradict our behavior. So pervasive and subtle is this lie that millions of professed believers have no clue that their lives belong in the dangerous category of 'hypocrite' (hypocrisy was the constant target of judgments uttered by Christ—Luke 12:56).

---

56 *You hypocrites! You know how to interpret the appearance of earth and sky, but why do you not know how to interpret the present time? Luke 12:56 ESV*

Biblical cosmology gives us a vantage point to see the soul-endangering absurdity of the divided life. For, Scripture urges us to offer our bodies to God as a living sacrifice (Rom 12;1-2). Thus, cosmology can assist us in **reasoning through the issue of sensual temptation and our required response of mortification of sin**. By 'divided life' we mean a soul-endangering disconnect between faith and practice (a wedge driven between what we say we believe and how we actually live).

In order to understand the lie of the divided life (and why it is against cosmology), **we begin at Satan's own Fall**. In effect, Lucifer's self-deceived reasoning was acted upon—the devil imagined that he 'won' his freedom and autonomy from God by rejecting his created purpose. His lie has now become his lifestyle. His imagined autonomy from God is founded on his rebellious act of attempting to transcend his created bounds and limitations. But here is where cosmology gives us an indispensable lens—Satan's rebellion did not create a new reality or new level of independent existence. What it did was put him in a death spiral. Like a planet knocked from of its orbit, Satan is careening toward a black purposeless eternity of wrath and crushing suffering.

The viewing of porn says in effect, "I accept Satan's cosmology in that I may take my yearnings for sex and for beauty outside of their divine boundaries and context." Thus porn is a false worldview which shatters and fragments God's good and wise creation structures (God's laws for social order). Porn deconstructs God's creation structures and jeopardizes our grasp of cosmology in the process. The knowledge of God is only retained when we have a unified life characterized by revering His creation structures found in cosmology.

Today's deception says, "I can rip God's good gifts out of their moral context and worship them and at the same time know and worship the one true God." Jesus says otherwise: no one can serve two masters. He will love one and hate the other. God refuses to let us successfully approach Him when we allow our heart idols to remain precious to us and unmoved (Ez 14:3-8ff.)

Either we love the truth of God and labor to conform our lives to that truth or we live by our natural desires and as a consequence, lose that truth (by distorting it, neglecting it, devaluing it, and suppressing it in order to justify the expression of our illicit yearnings). We need constant course corrections by the Word. Sin and guilt throw mud in our spiritual eyes—sin kills our objectivity in handling God's truth. The reason why is as follows: **in order for a person to retain his lusts, he must distort the truth** (because no one can live a radically dichotomized/divided lifestyle for long; either his behavior must change or the truth must be abandoned). Jesus described this truth-distorting activity as 'hating the light.' To do so is to prefer darkness (Jn 3:19-21).

God's creation structures are anchored in biblical cosmology which our culture is abandoning in the name of freedom. Consequently, we are nearing the precipice of destruction. To love pleasure more than God is to be part of this anarchy (2 Tim 3:4).

Treacherous, reckless, swollen with conceit, lovers of pleasure rather than lovers of God. 2 Tim 3:4 ESV

Let us remember, all sin is a resentment of God's moral majesty (Rom 8:6-8).

For to set the mind on the flesh is death, but to set the mind on the Spirit is life and peace. [7] For the mind that is set on the flesh is hostile to God, for it does not submit to God's law; indeed, it cannot. [8] Those who are in the flesh cannot please God. Romans 8:6-8 ESV

Sin patterns involve a rejection of our 'bounded-ness' (our created limits), which is a defiance of the wise and good limitations and boundaries God has placed upon us. Satan's lie about freedom says, "Liberty is freedom FROM divine design." God says that freedom is UNTO divine design (freedom is embracing His design for us in cosmology).

Our culture's sexual assault, posing as freedom, is so prolific that our moral sensibilities are disappearing. By our culture's mainstreaming of animal passions we are rapidly losing any sense of why God requires purity, decency, modesty, self-control, and fidelity. Once this stage is reached, a society becomes ignorant of the truth that God as holy Creator has an absolute claim upon our lives based upon His design for us. We lose sight of what we owe God by way of moral perfection and worship. Biblical cosmology asserts that God's character and God's purpose for the creation constitute prime reality.

Biblical cosmology defines the universe as a worshipping chorus of God—created to shine forth God's excellence, perfections, power, wisdom, and majesty. The social structures which God designed to govern mankind constitute a blueprint. Our loyalty to that blueprint is inseparable from our loyalty to God. We do not love, serve, and glorify God unless we fully embrace His creation structures—acknowledging that His righteous laws are designed to order the social institutions He created.

Marriage is the central social creation structure within cosmology. In other words, the normative units of a society are to be families. The biblical command to leave and cleave is central to growth in intimacy and commitment between the marriage partners (Gen 2:23-24). 'Bonding' or 'companion-ing' through sexual oneness is a biblical value that is a prerequisite for building strong marriages (Deut 24:5; Eph 5:25). The biblical counselor is always to impress upon the counselee that the Scriptures constantly call us to look to God in whom transformed relationships are possible. What God requires is beyond our natural capacities. The promise of the Word is that through the Holy Spirit's power, we may become by grace those who enjoy God-glorifying marriages.[1]

By divine design, God's gift of sexuality is intended to pull us out of ourselves and our self-occupied concerns and desires and "toward our spouse." The man committed to sexual purity is living in a state of sexual integrity toward his wife. In order to pursue their mutual pleasure in the marriage bed, the husband "is careful to live, to talk, to lead, and to love in such a way that his wife finds her fulfillment in giving herself to him in love." Their marital relations then become "the fulfillment of the entire relationship, and not an isolated physical act that is merely self-centered personal pleasure." "[T]his man can be confident that he is fulfilling his responsibilities both as a male and as a man. . . His sexual desires are being directed toward the one-flesh relationship that is the perfect paradigm of God's intention in creation."

The Porn Viewer

The porn viewer uses his sex drive as a dynamo of lust. In rejecting God's cosmology by turning to pornography, a man's desires are not turned toward a spouse, but are turned inward. His arousal through illicit images is tantamount to the seduction of the imagination and the corruption of his soul. This self-directed misuse of sexual desire becomes a 'tutorial' in selfishness. We are warned in 2 Peter 2:14 of a terrifying prospect—that by habitually sowing to lust it is possible to develop "a heart trained in greed." Al Mohler comments:

Pornography is a slander against the goodness of God's creation and a corruption of this good gift God has given His creatures out of His own self-giving love. To abuse this gift is to weaken, not only the institution of marriage, but the fabric of civilization itself. To choose lust over love is to debase humanity and to worship the false god Priapus in the most brazen form of idolatry. The deliberate use of pornography is nothing less than the willful invitation of illicit lovers and objectified sex objects. . . The damage to a man's heart is beyond measure, and the cost in human misery will only be made clear on the Day of Judgment.

What are the spiritual consequences of embracing Satan's cosmology? The use of hard-core pornography not only affects one's fellowship with God and with other believers, but also ultimately affects one's grasp of biblical theism. In other words, how one treats sexuality is inseparable from one's knowledge of God. Peter Jones notes that, "The masses are rendered insensate with a constant diet of sexual degradation, while at the same time, reassured by the spiritual and moral liberation that paganism offers." Jones argues that liberty of self-expression in the area of sexuality has historically been an instrument for the "deconstruction of the biblical God and sexuality."[3] No wonder Satan is so passionately committed to a cosmology that deconstructs God's plan for sex. The evil one knows that one cannot live as a sexual libertine and expect to keep his or her knowledge of God intact.

God's dominion mandate described in Psalm 8 extends to not only cultivating order in the physical creation, but also to the moral order which accompanies divinely ordained spiritual and social laws. This means that mankind is accountable to God for his stewardship of the creation structures governed by the laws of God. Now this is intensely relevant to fathers and husbands. For the man is the priest of his family—he is to raise up a God-fearing community in the 'miniature community' of his family. This is only possible if the husband has high praise and esteem for the wisdom, love and goodness of God manifested in divinely ordained creation structures (Deut 6:1-7).

Erotic Indulgence vs. the Big Picture

When we look intently at this cosmological truth of the dominion mandate, **it bursts us out of our privatized subjective view of religion.** Cosmology hits us with a revolutionary dose of reality by taking the issue of mortification of sin out of the truncated category of **'my own private heart piety,'** or 'my own private struggle with lust,' and placing it within God's master plan and design for creation and for society. Christian leader, Vishal Mangalwadi has said that, "Culture is made in the bedroom." By this he means that a man's sexuality has profound implications for the direction of society. A faithful husband who is true to his wife and provides for her will be a vital building block of society. On the other hand a man who makes pornography, or uses it, contributes to the tearing down of society.[4]

Here is the reason why: the husband and father is to exercise the dominion mandate in such a way that his marital fidelity becomes a culture-making act. A Christian marriage not defiled by the infidelity of erotic images sets the climate for culture-making to take place. Fidelity to Christ, fidelity to the marriage covenant, and fidelity to biblical cosmological design are inseparable! How we need to be blasted out of our shrunken perspective of private erotic indulgence. We need God's all-wise perspective—we need to stand atop the biblical vantage point of cosmology so that we might be staggered by the scope of God's purpose and plan.

The ancient lie is intended to overturn and destroy God's purpose for the creatures made in His image. Any acceptance of Satan's lie leads to idolatry. God's creation structures (such as heterosexual marriage) are at the heart of reality. The ancient lie sown in Eden suggested that God's design for mankind was a hindrance to personal fulfillment and free expression. But does man gain freedom by rejecting the bounds and limits inherent in God's design? We know the answer. When self becomes the reference point instead of Almighty God, man instantly becomes enslaved to idols. This is the loss of freedom.

Idolatry & the False Notion of Beauty

The evil one has never desisted from his efforts to deface the image of God by means of idolatry. The worship of created things is idolatry. This is how the devil further shatters the image of God. Idolatry destroys our human unity and by contrast the worship of God in Christ strengthens our humanness. Sexual idolatry is a dysfunction in worship. Whatever we worship in place of God places us into bondage and servitude. The way out through Christ entails embracing a unified Christian experience firmly anchored in biblical cosmology. Only when our lives are aligned with God's prescriptions for our social relations will God be glorified in us.

Idolatry is tied to false notions of beauty. Scripture imbues upon us that beauty has no existence independent of God. True beauty is always joined to divinely ordained transcendentals of truth, purpose, moral context, design, covenant, goodness, wisdom, and order. Biblically, beauty is to serve as a glory pointer. Beauty joined to the transcendentals does just that—it directs us to higher things—to the honor of God who is the source and standard of true beauty. Beauty divorced from the divine context of transcendentals is idolatrous—it cannot serve as a glory pointer.

For this reason beauty is the most extensive battle ground for the eternal souls of men and women. The devil traps and enslaves through idolatry by removing beauty from divine transcendentals. **The enemy offers beauty by itself, as if it can stand alone without serving as a glory pointer.** Satan is the great compartmentalizer. By ripping beauty and pleasure out of their God-given contexts, he fragments our understanding of life —he fractures our understanding of God's design for creation— and he does so in order to fragment and fracture human idolaters (thereby further defacing the image of God in man).

Through doctrines of demons and the lying philosophies of the world, he blinds men to cosmology and shrinks God's domain in the world to a tiny religious sphere so that he as the deceiver may use the whole of creation for his idolatrous purposes. How do we escape idolatry? We must insist upon the truth; that every square inch of our experience belongs to God. Cosmology gives us that big picture. The depth of what we love on earth we must love for Christ's sake, for all things exist for Him. They exist for our enjoyment, but ultimately to show His excellence and goodness.

The evil one **seeks to shipwreck the faith of many professed believers** by suggesting to them that their Christianity **is safe in a partitioned off compartment in their lives.** This is a deadly lie because true faith is a constant whole-souled act. All the faculties of our being are called upon to live in genuine faith in Christ. And not the least of these faculties of our being is our affections. Jonathan Edwards stressed that the religious affections are the fruit of a new heart, and that these affections are what moves the Christian life like a watch spring.[5] Biblical cosmology gives us a high enough vantage to actually see how God's universe works.

The Holy Spirit takes up residence forever in the true child of God and confirms to His child that God's glory and our happiness are bound up together. Satan cannot counterfeit this sentiment—no natural man sees God's glory and the creature's happiness woven together in Christ. The hypocrite, says Edwards, speculates about spiritual things whereas the soul of the truly converted feeds upon spiritual truths, upon Christ's perfect suitability to save.[6] The true believer is always growing in his affection for divine holiness, and as a consequence his disgust for what is unholy grows.[7] Strong love for Christ expresses itself in fruitfulness, self-denial, and mortification of our lusts.[8]

Edwards shows us why a compartmentalized Christian life is impossible for any extended length of time. True Christianity is bound up in the believer's religious affections. Christ will not share our hearts with idols. As we have been stating, God's creation structures are just as real as our own solar system. At the end of creation week God pronounced His benediction upon every creational structure; declaring them all to be exceedingly good (Gen. 1:31).

God's blessing of His creation structures includes all of the relations which He has sanctioned, including social relations. **Our problem is that we tend to view his moral laws (including his laws governing social structures) as separated from cosmology.** We tend to buy into postmodernity's lie that God's laws for social structures are but arbitrary impositions of the church upon society rather than what they really are. These laws are creation structures; the very moral fabric of the universe, the very foundation of freedom and dignity, and the bedrock support of a just society and an ordered civilization. Biblical cosmology alone gives us a high enough vantage to actually see how God's universe works.

The gospel enables us to obey God from the heart—to live unto God's cosmology—to "be" the image of God and thereby reflect our Creator. The gospel is intended to radically transform us by getting our affections wrapped around things above. It is all about spiritual seeing; about true source and true treasure. The gospel puts us in God's story. It roots us into His plot so that His glory and our good are bound up together in the Person of Christ.

Our whole lives then become an answer to God's call. We could say that the gospel writes a new 'script' for us by transferring us out of the kingdom of darkness and into the kingdom of God's Son and by making us adopted sons of God who are born from above (Gal 4:57). Those who have believed savingly live out their new identity in Christ. That new life lived out is the warranty, proof, and evidence of possessing saving grace. The gospel pours the new believer into its 'mould'—giving precise shape to our new life direction in Christ.

A Christian man must find his place in the battle of the ages as it is a battle for 'all the marbles'—for the eternal souls of men and women. Central in this battle is the human body with the very epicenter being the sexual body. One's body, with its sexuality, is intended by God to be a prime spiritual resource. The body is not for immorality, but for the Lord (1 Cor 6:13). Our body is either presented to the Lord each day, or it is presented to unrighteousness. So crucial is the human body (with its sexuality) to the battle of the ages that Paul commands his readers not to go on presenting the members of their body as weapons of unrighteousness. Instead present yourselves to God as those alive from the dead, and your members as weapons of righteousness to God (Rom 6:11-13).

Biblical cosmology gives us a vantage point to see that our lives constitute a kind of biography under construction. God will read each person's 'biography' aloud on judgment day (Rom 2:16). What a sobering thought that we are becoming today what we will be tomorrow. Each person's life will ultimately prove to be an object lesson to the watching universe. God will bring history to its consummation in Christ, and then history will prove to be an exhaustive lesson—declaring to the rational universe the results of honoring God and the consequences of not honoring God. Would we live any differently if we were convinced of cosmology's message that my life will prove to be an object lesson to the rational universe, either a message of eternal honor or eternal dishonor?

AUDIO 2.1 Biblical Cosmology Summary

Jay Wegter speaks on the cosmology chapter, summarizing and preparing readers for the next section: **Fear of the Lord and the Cross.**

Review Questions

1) What does biblical cosmology have to do with our relationships?
2) Why is a divided life so dangerous?
3) How did the lie in Eden produce a false view of our bodies?
4) What does cosmology have to do with us living as the image of God?

Chapter Notes

1) In biblical cosmology we learn that God has a specific plan or 'blueprint' for mankind. Our Creator's plan for us includes His purposes for our bodies. Therefore this 'blueprint' affects all of our relationships.
2) God's plan is good and wise and loving, and when we embrace His plan for us it becomes the basis for human dignity, joy, fulfillment, and flourishing.
3) Problem: when we set aside the divine plan (biblical cosmology), the consequence is a *divided life* in which spirituality is divorced from God's blueprint for our relationships and our bodies. A divided life opens the door to a host of sins including porn use.
4) This may be shocking, but a divided life is actually the devil's cosmology. Here is the reason why, the evil one's cosmology says: "I may use the creation and my body and the bodies of others the way I wish, all without consequences."
5) The satanic Lie whispered in the Garden of Eden offered mankind independence from God's plan found in His Word. This resulted in a false view of our bodies, sexuality, and beauty. Since the entrance of the lie, people have demanded for themselves the role of deciding how their bodies and creation are to be used. This false view of freedom can only be reversed by the Gospel.
6) God is rescuing millions from the 'shipwreck' of a divided life. Through redemption in Christ believing sinners may enjoy a

unified Christian experience in which they live as the *image of God*. Joy is the blessed result of allowing God's plan to define our entire life.

7) The Christian's obedience is much more than merely seeking to stay out of trouble. We are appointed by God to be caretakers of the spiritual and moral order found in His blueprint. The growing believer, enabled by Christ, wants to live out his or her part in the plan of God. That means living according to God's good, wise, and loving commands and boundaries.

Endnotes:

1 Hindson and Eyrich, "Totally Sufficient," pp. 195-197
2 Al Mohler, "The Seduction of Pornography," p. 3
3 Peter Jones, "Androgyny: The Pagan Sexual Ideal," Americans for Truth about Homosexuality, p.6
4 Vishal Mangalwadi, "Must the Sun set on the West?"
5 Jonathan Edwards, The Religious Affections, pp. 28-31
6 Ibid, pp. 166-167, 172-173, 197-198, 200
7 Ibid, p. 317
8 Ibid, pp. 352-354, 371, 374-375

Jay Wegter

Section 2

Fear of the Lord and the Cross

Section Objectives

1. To learn how the cross of Christ shows us our helplessness and the futility of trying to be accepted by God through our works.

2. To learn why the fear of God is necessary if one is to truly affirm God's justice.

3. To welcome being humbled by the cross as it strips us bare of all self-righteousness—only then will we flee to Christ as our only refuge.

4. To learn why God is glorified when we are 'righteous by faith in Christ' alone.

5. To understand that the cross prepares the way for all truly good works.

Fear of the Lord and the Cross

Adapted from: Gerhard O. Forde, On being a Theologian of the Cross, Reflections on Luther's Heidelberg Disputation, 1518, Eerdmans, 1997, and adapted from: Gardiner Spring, The Attraction of the Cross, Banner of Truth, 1983.

A. The cross is a monument to the world that man deserves to die (Gardiner Spring). The intensity of our moral depravity and the infinite demerit of our sin are taught by the cross. Only man's rebellion against God could have justified the sacrifice of the eternal Son of God. The cross shows us man's helplessness and depravity [1] (Is 53:4-9; Gal 3:22).

Man's state is hopeless without the cross. The eternal Son of God **was smitten by the sword of divine justice** *in the 'room and place' of man.* This lesson the cross teaches us is repulsive to sinners—it offends because it convicts us of our sinfulness and of our **ill desert** (what we deserve). The cross is the proof of human guilt inscribed in blood. [2]

The cross is the great divider of men in this life and the afterlife. God's wrath is satisfied toward the believer, but inextinguishable fury will burn against that man who disowns the substitution of God's Son and nothing can protect him from coming wrath (Heb 2: 1-3; 10:26-31). [3]

MOVIE 2.2 Fear of the Lord and the Cross

Understanding why the fear of God is so critically important in a relationship with Him.

²Therefore we must pay much closer attention to what we have heard, lest we drift away from it. ² For since the message declared by angels proved to be reliable, and every transgression or disobedience received a just retribution, ³ how shall we escape if we neglect such a great salvation? It was declared at first by the Lord, and it was attested to us by those who heard. Heb. 2:1-3 ESV

B. The cross, by showing a man's ill desert, reveals the human condition. The cross kills our optimism that man can be improved. The perennial 'theology' of our fallen race is one of human potential. The cross says the opposite: that we are condemned, that **the Fall wrecked our humanity and left it floating like debris** on the surface of the ocean. The cross 'cure' is drastic; it slays the hope of survival of self. Our natural carnal religious optimism suggests that we have the ability to place our feet on the 'river bottom' of our depravity and walk upstream against the current. We instinctively assume that we must try to do our best and that God will make up for our shortcomings. [4] Scripture tells us that the way of the law is a dead end, *"the law is not of faith"* (Gal 3:12).

By the Cross of Christ our Religious 'instincts' are Overturned.

A. The cross reveals our best works as deadly sins. Not just dead works, but 'deadly works' because **they keep us from total trust in Christ.** *"How much more will the blood of Christ, who through the eternal Spirit offered Himself without blemish to God, cleanse your conscience from dead works to serve the living God?"* (Heb 9:14). Our good works (prior to salvation) are deadly sins because they cause us to defend against naked trust in the mercy of God. **'Good works' prior to salvation actually work against unconditional grace.** As men we naturally love trusting an 'arm of flesh.' Prior to salvation, any trust in our works blocks full reliance upon the sovereign compassion of God in Christ. [5]

---

[14] How much more will the blood of Christ, who through the eternal Spirit offered himself without blemish to God, purify our conscience from dead works to serve the living God. Heb. 9:14 ESV

The cross of Christ is intended to kill our religious aspirations. *"For not knowing about God's righteousness, and seeking to establish their own,* **they did not subject themselves to the righteousness of God. For Christ is the end of the law for righteousness to everyone that believes"** (Rom 10:3-4). Luther argues that deadly sins are found in pious places. Our works entice us away from bare trust in God's mercy. Thus, works are deadly sins where there is not the fear of God. The fear of God keeps us from trusting in our works and attempting to make them a support of the soul. The cross of Christ slays self-assurance because genuine fear of God **causes a man to be pleased with God, not with self.** *"Therefore, the Law has become our tutor to lead us to Christ, that we may be justified by faith"* (Gal 2:24). [6]

---

[24]And those who belong to Christ Jesus have crucified the flesh with its passions and desires. Gal 2:24 ESV

B. Man's religious sensibilities of 'self-help' are demolished by the cross of Christ. "Do your best and God will do the rest." This slogan does not seem pernicious on the surface, but it is spiritually deadly to the soul. Perhaps the reason why we do not recognize that this slogan is hostile to the cross of Christ is because the church today is so weak on the gospel.

In natural religion, we instinctively assume that we must try to do our best and that God will make up for our shortcomings. [7] Natural religion suggests that our works make us fit objects of divine mercy. The false professor of Christianity *appears to trust in*

Christ alone, but his profession is in word only, and not in heart. Secretly he cleaves to his own righteousness. The cross shows the wickedness involved in self-trust, evincing that person's hostility to God's free salvation.

But why would a religious sinner oppose free salvation in Christ? The answer is that the self-righteous man is reluctant to be under obligation to Christ alone (owing all to Him for time and eternity). The preference of the natural man, contends Gardiner Spring, is to rely on his own wretched performances over the great work of Jesus the Lord. [8]

Common distortions of the gospel assume that Christ's righteousness is infused into us (imparted to us or transferred to us so that we become acceptable to God). This is NOT the   justification purchased by Christ's finished work on the cross. The biblical gospel teaches that the true believer is treated as righteous NOT due to infused righteousness but because Christ his   covenant Head is righteous. This makes all the difference in the world. For Christ's righteousness is an *alien* righteousness which is imputed to believers (set to their account). God justifies through faith alone. The cross of Christ furnished this completed justification. This is why God accepts believing sinners —there is no other way for your cause to be good. Faith in the cross is faith in God's testimony concerning His Son. God cannot lie (Heb 6:17-20). He is the Author of the cross and its accomplishments (Jn 3:16-21). [9]

C. It is easy, even for religious men, to reject the testimony God has given concerning His Son. Our Fallen race is naturally inclined to reject the testimony God has given because *the cross contains principles which are at war with the idolatry of self.* As long as the sinner's selfishness, pride, and love of sinning are undisturbed, he will resist God's testimony concerning the cross. Selfishness, pride, and love of sinning must receive a deadly wound from the cross. Only then will the person confide in God. [10]

The impenitent, stubborn heart battles against the conviction of the Spirit. There is no more fierce or severe struggle. The Spirit's quickening power brings the elect sinner low and makes him willing to exercise dutiful, penitent, humble, submissive faith in the cross. He goes from an enemy to a friend of God. [11]

D. To trust in the cross alone for salvation is to repudiate all other proposed places of refuge. Gardiner Spring observes that whenever a man has been awakened to the danger of sin by the Spirit of God, no matter that person's background (cultural or religious), that man will embrace the unqualified conviction that *the cross is his only hiding place.* And with that conviction comes the utmost horror of all former refuges of lies (Is 28:14-22). Saving faith reaches up to the cross in an exercise of both intellect and affection. The will consents and that person suddenly regards all former refuges as lies, false hopes, and as worthless as spider webs. *"I know whom I have believed and I am convinced that **He is able** to guard what I have entrusted to Him **until that day**"* (2 Tim 1:12).[12]

Where there is no Fear of God, Men retain their Controversy with God.

A. The cross brings a redemption which presupposes that the sinner deserves eternal death. Men will admit that they are sinners, but they have no inward sense of measure of their ill desert (what they deserve from God's justice). They do not (and cannot) feel it would be right for God to inflict upon them this terrible eternal doom of perdition. Thus, every man who **lacks the fear of God has a quarrel or controversy with God concerning what sin deserves.** Only when by the illumination of the Spirit will men reflect on who God is and who they are in themselves. Only then will they have fewer difficulties with eternal punishment.[13]

B. The reality of our ill desert due to sin is a withering and alarming subject. It elicits shame, blame, and embarrassment. It crushes and brings a person low. **The mind**

naturally revolts, considering it to be a 'conflict of interest' to dwell upon the turpitude of their crimes against heaven. The controversy with God is a pitched battle over the issue of what personal sin deserves. Men remain God's enemies because they hate His inflexible justice. They **cannot bear** the truth that **God is right and man is terribly wrong**. Man's bias keeps him disguising, discounting, and covering his sin and running from the enormity of his guilt before God (Prov 28:13).

13 Whoever conceals his transgressions will not prosper, but he who confesses and forsakes them will obtain mercy. Prov 28:13 ESV

When he hears about the holiness and justice of God, a conflagration erupts in his conscience. If his iniquity were displayed comprehensively but for a moment, he would cry out for the rocks to Fall upon him rather than face God: *"And the kings of the earth and the great men and the commanders and the rich and the strong and every slave and free man, **hid themselves in the caves** and among the rocks of the mountains; and **they said to the mountains** and to the rocks, '**Fall on us and hide us from** the presence of **Him** who sits on the throne, and from the wrath of the Lamb; for the great day of their wrath has come; and **who is able to stand**"* (Rev 6:15-17)? The sinner (while the controversy remains) prefers no God to the doctrine of a God who **threatens man with hell**.[14]

The Fear of God causes the Sinner to place his Hope in the Cross.

A. The fear of God utterly slays self-assurance. The awakened sinner comes to understand that *if God should mark iniquities—who could stand?* (Ps 130:3). If God's wrath is kindled, you are gone (Ps 2:12; Jer 15:14).

---

[12] Kiss the Son, lest he be angry, and you perish in the way, for his wrath is quickly kindled. Blessed are all who take refuge in him. Psalm 2:12 ESV

As long as a person comforts himself that his works are only dead and not deadly, he continues to **offend God** and draws glory away from Him. By contrast, **the fear of God decries any saving merit in our works**, and is therefore inseparable from ongoing naked trust in His mercy through Christ. This trust involves continual rejection of all creaturely support and consolation in one's works. Holiness and divine law seal off all pious-religious escape routes. Faith in the cross means that all our security is from God alone and his forgiveness. *"But there is forgiveness with Thee, that Thou may be feared"* (Ps 130:4). [15]

B. It takes the cross to shock us into seeing the hopelessness and bankruptcy of self-reliance—only then will we take responsibility for sin. While a person is doing what he is *in himself*, he sins and seeks himself in everything. Man, by his own will, *CANNOT* prepare himself for grace. Attempts to do so are a denial of God's power to save. Doing one's best (and relying on it) means that the will is yet bound to self (Luke 18:9-14). The Law of God '*cross-examines*' us so that we might despair of a solution in ourselves and be 'cross-justified' (Gal 3:22-27). Only the gospel of the cross can take us off of self and transfer our trust **from self to Christ**. [16]

C. God can only be known by means of the cross. Only those 'bankrupted' of self-righteousness receive grace. As men who wish to know God, we must be brought to a place where we utterly despair of our own ability. Any speck of trust in *doing our best* and we have not despaired. God refuses to be known except by the cross. God 'hides Himself' in the cross and refuses to be known any other way. [17]

D. God makes Himself known through the cross first of all by crucifying our self-righteousness. The natural man feels he must do his best—as if his efforts can play a part in mollifying God, placating God, and in some ways obligating God. Carnal supports of the soul aim at **winning God's favor and repairing the self.** These efforts are all doomed to fail. All cross-less, grace-less religion amounts to nothing more than sinful man **imagining he can do something to protect himself and find safety from the terror of divine majesty.** Any confidence in carnal supports of the soul gives evidence that a person does not know God (nor truly fears Him so as to flee to Christ alone for refuge). [18]

As believing Men, we need to know what the Cross does to us.

A. Before we can see God in the cross we must see ourselves in the cross. This means that the cross functions first as a 'mirror'. God conceals His divine majesty in the cross. He works sub-contrario in the cross—that is He works through abject weakness which is contrary to His reasoned attributes of strength (Paul Zahl, A Short Systematic Theology, pp. 28, 33, 36). The net effect is to arrest us, to kill our religious aspirations, for the cross reveals our best works as deadly sins. We are startled by the cross to find that sin has been multiplied through our supposed morality; for the law makes sinners worse and it makes them proud and presumptuous. The law does not improve sinners. The law way of finding God is a dead end street (Rom 10:1-4) The cross is designed to make us despair of our natural moral and religious powers (Rom 3:19-20; 8:2-4; 5:20-21; 7:13ff.). [20]

To be face to face with the message of the cross is unnerving. Your conscience can no longer defend you. You look in the 'mirror' of the cross and you behold the fact that your sins have done this. We will only see God in the cross when we first see self in the 'mirror' of the cross. Luther explains this as follows:

You are the one who is torturing Christ thus, for your sins have surely wrought this . . . Therefore when you see the nails piercing Christ's hands, you can **be certain that it is your work**. When you behold the crown of thorns, you may rest assured **these are your evil thoughts**, etc. [21]

The Reformer's point is this: that the cross closes in on us so we understand we are crucified with Christ. His story becomes our story. The cross cure is drastic—**it has to kill you before it can make you alive**. [22]

B. The cross doesn't just inform, it attacks and afflicts us. The knowledge of God comes when "God does Himself to us."[23] In other words, because *we are sinners, God can only be known through suffering*. The false god of natural religion is constructed around our projects (our resolutions and moral reformations). We invent a god who is amendable to our designs and goals and then we solicit his compliance. The God of Scripture is the polar opposite of the human improvement scheme—He strikes at our usual religious aspirations which we attempt under the wisdom of the law. By means of the cross, He demolishes our religious sensibilities. We feel naked, exposed, flushed out of hiding. Our instinctive response is to *want to return to the 'safety' of doing something*[24].

The natural man (unregenerate man) regards his moral and spiritual state much as an athlete does his game, "I just have to work on a couple of principles here; I can compensate; I can do this." The cross comes to extinguish the religious desires and fleshly optimism of the old Adam and Eve—

to show us the utter ineptitude of our will in pleasing and knowing God by law. Resentment and a turbulent conscience arise when our religious sensibilities are attacked. This is why the cross offends—men love the opposite of the cross. **They want man-centered natural wisdom, man's glory, human power**, and human deeds. The cross exposes all of these false integration points as **idolatrous**.[25]

The cross proclaims that God is the Governor of the world and that He is right and we are wrong. Every true Christian on every continent acquiesces to the rectitude of the penalty evidenced in the cross—God is right and we are terribly wrong, **"I deserve eternal death!"** By means of the cross, the proud heart of the sinner is humbled; he accepts the punishment of his iniquity revealed in the gospel. He submits to God. Then, and only then, his controversy with God terminates, for the believer truly approves God's sentence. There can be no acceptance of the gospel while the sinner quarrels with God's justice and God's law. To oppose God's precepts and penalties is to be a stranger to divine mercy. [26]

C. The cross of Christ pierces our ego-driven, self-justifying motivations. The cross always brings us back to the freeness of God in bestowing grace. It takes us back to our utter inability to obligate God (Rom 11:33-36). When we feed on the truth of the cross it keeps us in a posture of dependency. And for good reason! Ongoing faith in Christ involves repeatedly consenting to have Christ labor for us, in our place, and as our Substitute, so that God can be infinitely kind to us for Christ's sake and not our own. The gospel enthroned in conscience **keeps us** in that frame of mind where we **continually consent to have Christ represent us**. I have chosen the word "consent" because, like the apostle Peter, we must *consent* (against inner resistance) to have Christ stoop so low as to **wash the filth** from our person. This is our preparation for good works that glorify God.

The Cross is vitally related to our Good Works.

A. Good works begin only when by the cross the old Adam is put to death and the new man appears (2 Cor 5:17; Col 3:10). The cross must slay the old man's fleshly orientation: 'that by good works one is going to become righteous.' The cross reverses everything, giving us new values, for Christ is the Creator of the new man (our works cannot make a new man). Christ is *the Architect, the Builder, and the Blueprint* of the new man (Col 3:10).

---

[10]and have put on the new self, which is being renewed in knowledge after the image of its creator. [11] Here there is not Greek and Jew, circumcised and uncircumcised, barbarian, Scythian, slave, [e] free; but Christ is all, and in all. Cor 3:10 ESV

Being righteous before God without works clears the way for practical holiness. When the reality of justification sinks in, preposterous joy hits us; a new day dawns when we understand by the Spirit that the righteousness we have in Christ is complete in itself. It is like the joy and ecstasy of being in love. Justification in Christ is all-sufficient. *"But to the one who does not work, but believes in Him who justifies the ungodly, **his faith is reckoned as righteousness**"* (Rom 4:5). [27]

B. Now in Christ, good works are God's works in the believer (Eph 2:10; Gal 2:20). We have all we need in Christ because faith restored by grace plants all new motives in us. **A good work is good only IF it is done out of faith, hope, and love.** The cross of Christ takes away the possibility of doing something meritorious before God. The power to do good comes from the wild claim that everything has already been done in Christ. ***None of our works now affect our acceptance with God*** —Christ dwells in us by faith and works through us (Gal 2:20). [28]

---

[20] By the blood of the eternal covenant, [21] equip you with everything good that you may do his will, working in us that which is pleasing in his sight, through Jesus Christ, to whom be glory forever and ever. Amen. Heb 13:20-21 ESV

C. The believer is aroused to work through living faith in Christ's work. In the gospel order, the impetus to do good works comes entirely from being moved, aroused, and motivated by the completed work of Christ who **dwells in the believer through faith**. Says Luther, "Deeds of mercy are aroused by the works **through** which Christ saved us."

Those who find their all and all in Christ are motivated to be imitators of God. *"Therefore be imitators of God, as beloved children; and walk in love, just as Christ also loved you and gave Himself up for us, an offering and sacrifice to God as a fragrant aroma"* (Eph 5:1-2). It was Augustine who said that Christ must first be a sacrament for us *before* He can be an example. His point is that our motive to walk as Jesus did will only be true *if* Christ is our righteousness, status, standing, favor, sonship, and acceptance before God. But, in all non-evangelical forms of Christendom the order is inverted; Christ is an example to follow first. And, in so doing, human works are made a support of the soul. [29]

'The Truth of the Cross is our only Theology' (Luther).

A. In contrast to instinctive religion, the cross differs from all other methods of changing man. The cross does not attempt to harness natural inclinations. The cross works **AGAINST** natural inclinations. The cross alone can make us fit for God and heaven. It considers nothing accomplished until the living God has **displaced every idol in the soul**. When the cross does its work, a man has a united heart—his double-mindedness has been replaced with single-minded loyalty to his God. The cross secures this change. Of course this is another reason why unsaved men hate the cross; it is utterly clear concerning God's sole ownership of us. [30]

B. The power, wisdom, and truth of the cross are seen in the following insights:
- Its intrinsic excellence as the power and wisdom of God
- Its binding obligations to believe and follow Christ
- Its perfect fitness to reverse man's ruin
- Its effectiveness in securing **everlasting life beyond the grave**
- Its power to attach the conscience to confidence in the Son
- Its ability to **give the knowledge of self and of God**

C. Every true believer knows what a battle it is 'to labor to enter His rest' (Heb 4:11). It is no small effort to consistently enjoy gospel rest in Christ and to make the 'verdict' of heaven at Calvary the verdict of one's conscience. Everything seems to war against that heavenly verdict: the world, the flesh, the devil, and even religion. Each of these pushes for personal performance, measuring up, and achievement as the ground and basis for quieting the conscience. The conscience is a tireless researcher, always collecting evidence of our moral failures and shortcomings. It looks into the smallest details of a person's life, examining motives and intents of the heart, and frequently accuses the individual of transgressions in the thought life. Our great temptation is to do what is wholly natural to us—namely to do the bookkeeping of conscience by means of law.

In the law approach to conscience management, the individual argues for peace of conscience from the vantage point of strengths and performance—**as if achievements have the**

power to outweigh demerits. So engrained is the attempt to **quiet the conscience by means of law,** one may accurately say that 'law works' is the religion with which   we were born. It comes natural to us. We are all self-justifiers by nature (Luke 10:29; 16:15). When law is on the throne of conscience there is an accompanying 'lowering of the market' in regards to God's requirements. In other words, **the bar is lowered to the capabilities of carnal man.** It is a patent refusal to submit to God's righteousness evidenced in the cross of Christ (Rom 10:3). It is an attempt to placate the conscience and offset guilt by appealing to the moral value of things that are humanly achievable.

CONCLUSION:

How you view your Christian character (your ability to view it objectively or not) is revealed in how you treat the cross. The cross is the test of character. Christ is appointed for the rise and Fall of many (Luke 2:34). To reject the cross is to be an enemy of God (Phil 3:18-19). Friends of the cross are those who love God's character, hate their sin, and therefore serve God. The godly renounce every other confidence but the cross of Christ. Their sole dependence is upon Christ who is able to save them to the uttermost (Heb 7:25-26). Thus, the cross is the test that reveals a person's source of trust for salvation.[31]

REVIEW QUESTIONS:

1) How does the cross of Christ give us power to resist sin? (HINT: Christ died to set us free from the rule of sin. And Christ's death gives us a perfect standing before God.)

2) How does the cross of Christ give us the proper motives for good works now that we are saved?

3) Why is the cross of Christ a good test of character? (HINT: how do we value the cross in our Christian walk? Does the cross cause us to love both God's justice and mercy?)

AUDIO 2.2 Fear of the Lord and the Cross Summary

Tap the audio to begin listening to the professor discuss the subject. For those on the print version, spin up your DVDs to "Audio Recording 2.2".

Endnotes:

1 Gardiner Spring, The Attraction of the Cross, Banner of Truth, 1983. p. 26

2 Ibid, 206-207

3 Ibid, p. 28

4 Gerhard O. Forde, On being a Theologian of the Cross, Reflections on Luther's Heidelberg Disputation, 1518, Eerdmans, 1997, p. 18

5 Ibid, pp. 32-33, 37

6 Ibid, pp. 38-40

7 Ibid, p. 24

8 Spring, p. 54

9 Ibid, pp. 92-96, 99

10 Ibid, p. 104

11 Ibid, pp. 10, 113

12 Ibid, pp. 38, 100

13 Ibid, pp. 129, 133

14 Ibid, p. 134-137, 147-148

15 Forde, pp. 42-47

16 Ibid, pp. 50, 54, 58-59

17 Ibid, pp. 5-66, 80

18 Ibid, pp. 79-82

19 Paul Zahl, A Short Systematic Theology, pp. 28, 33, 36

20 Ibid, pp. 25-26, 31-32

21 Forde, pp. 7-8, 77

22 Ibid, pp. 13-15

23 Ibid, p. 90

24 Ibid, pp. 88-90, 93

25 Ibid, pp. 93, 99

26 Ibid, pp. 148-150

27 Ibid, pp. 104-106

28 Ibid, pp. 109-111

29 Ibid, pp. 111-112

30 Spring, p. 305

31 Ibid, pp. 205, 209, 306

Section 3

Genesis, Gender and Sexuality

Section Objectives

1. In the areas of gender and sexuality: to learn greater discernment as we study the radically opposing answers given by popular culture versus the Bible.

2. To become very familiar with how God expects our bodies to be used so that we may better obey Him.

3. To understand the great beauty in the redemptive analogy of marriage (Christ and the church) and to realize what God's gift of marriage says to the world about our Savior and about us as believers.

4. To be able to recognize and avoid the prevailing lies in our culture about gender and sexuality.

The Doctrine of Creation and Gender

God's Word is perfectly clear about His design for male and female—it is a glorious vision for union in marriage and community in family unit and in society. Our culture is sending a different message which is intended to overturn God's blueprint for man and woman and family.

Now, what a person believes about origins (or, how the universe got here) has everything to do with how one views the subject of gender. Those who subscribe to Darwinism suggest that the universe is but a chance explosion and chaotic collision of dust and gas that somehow produced order and information. Under the evolutionary view of origins, mankind has no real innate significance. Humans are regarded as evolutionary latecomers whose appearance intruded upon a world already filled with creatures occupying every conceivable ecological niche.

Our desire to glorify God ought to be inseparable from our purpose to declare the truth of the divine vision for male and female. But, in order to better understand how God's plan is under attack this chapter will expose our culture's prevailing lies about gender. In regard to the lies which permeate our society, perhaps you have heard the term, "culture war?" It is defined as a clash between two mutually exclusive worldviews—God's view of the world found in the Bible, and Satan's view of the world found in secularism and in false philosophies and false religion.

These two opposing worldviews (biblical and secular) have a radically different understanding of man's place in the universe. Darwinistic pantheism (which makes the divine a part of the created universe) says that the universe has no real meaning, and that male and female is but a coincidence of nature. You can automatically see how this view sends the message that you may do what you please with your human body: enhance it, deface it, neglect it, color it, pierce it, eroticize it, drug it, stimulate it, worship it—after all, it is but a blank canvas on which you depict or establish the identity of your choice.

Darwinism is at War with God

Obviously Darwinism is at war with what God says about our purpose as men and women under God—and the role of male and female is central in God's plan. By contrast, evolutionary theory is not empirical science—and when it moves from a theory of origins to a dogmatic view of the nature of reality, it has become a religious philosophy and not scientific at all.

Instead of an accident called the **'Big Bang' Scripture** tells us that it was the Word of our infinite God that called the universe into existence (Ps 33:6). Now God did **not** need to make the universe because He was lonely; the three sublime Beings of the Godhead for all eternity past dwelled in a community of **perfect love, happiness, respect, and communication.**

Thus we learn from Scripture that God wills to be known. **The creation is a revelation of God,** whereas **Scripture and the Christ, the Word of God incarnate, is the special revelation of God.** Now God created two orders of creatures (beings) who would find their highest pleasure and purpose in Him—people and angels. Both orders of creatures are designed to run on God so to speak, to be lost in wonder, praise, adoration, and awe of their Maker.

The creation exists to praise God. And central to that plan of creation glorifying God is the role of human beings—the only order of creatures made in the image and likeness of God. That means that **when our lives are ordered according to His infallible Word; God is glorified and we are joyous.**

Creation Structures

As Designer and Maker, He has given us categories, relations, boundaries, and names which describe the intended functions of what He has made. **We refer to these as "creation structures."** These creation structures form God's basic blueprint for His moral, rational creation. God ordained the institution of marriage—heterosexual marriage is a creation structure. Family is a creation structure. The moral law of God found in The Ten Commandments is a creation structure.

Just as the organs of your body have a function to perform according to their unique design; so also does male and female and the way that they relate to one another. God's great gift of marital, sexual oneness was given in a moral context —a covenant if you will, the covenant of marriage. Now the whole animate creation is designed to operate within the functional boundaries and purposes God has set.

In the world of animals, or non-human creatures, function follows form (or bodily design)—kangaroos glorify God by hopping, eagles by soaring, cheetahs by sprinting. **Everything God has made falls into categories that He has established,** and each one has specific functions. Our own moon has a function that glorifies God; it not only is the earth's 'night light' it also creates the ocean tides, sets the reproductive calendars of countless creatures, and renews the freshness of bays and lagoons by tides and currents.

Now according to Scripture, **God has wise and just laws which are to govern us**—the creatures made in His image. God's commandments are meant to keep us living in accordance with our created purpose. So purpose, order, design, and function are all joined together in the infinitely wise and good laws God has given us.

Part of God's law as revealed in creation shows what the roles of male and female are in regard to each other. Eve was made to be Adam's helpmate (Gen. 1:20). **She was Adam's perfect complement in every way, in gender role, in emotions, and in anatomy.** This concept is known as "complementariety." Biblical cosmology drives our doctrine of gender and the complementary roles. However, our culture is waging war against these two. It is trying to remove the differences between male and female **by not celebrating the God-ordained differences.**

Since the fall into sin the human race has always been at war against the knowledge of God according to Romans 1:18ff.

---

[18]*For the wrath of God is revealed from heaven against all ungodliness and unrighteousness of men, who by their unrighteousness suppress the truth. Romans 1:18 ESV*

But, what is interesting is the way in which sinful man attacks the knowledge of God. Sinners do so by attacking God's design for man and woman. However, our design as men and women comes from being made in the image of God. Our identity finds itself in this truth. **The spirit of our age is engaged in promoting a naturalistic materialistic view of the universe**—as if the universe made itself, upholds itself, and interprets itself. This is an attempt to explain the creation by the creation instead of by the Creator.

The philosophy of naturalism **destroys the truth of man and woman as the image of God.** This of course removes God's blueprint for man and woman and flings the door open to make our choices based upon **animal passions**—and then calling our yielding to those passions, lusts and instincts, **"freedom."**

That is precisely where we are as a culture. Freedom is now being defined as throwing off divine constraints. The Word of God defines freedom as the very opposite—it is power to live within the boundaries of God's all-wise plan and design for us.

A Spiritual War drives the Culture War

The culture war that is raging between biblical family values and sexual immorality is **not merely a conflict between opposing sets of values.** The culture war conceals a spiritual war just beneath its surface. **It is a spiritual war because the knowledge of God is at stake,** the eternal souls of men and women are at stake, and the preservation of our civilization is at stake.

The culture war is a spiritual war, and at the epicenter of the worldview battle is the human body. Thus how one uses his or her gender and sexuality **is a powerful declaration of their worldview.** The human body is the battlefield. How you use your body determines who your master is and what your worldview is.

How well the powers of darkness know this. Spiritually, they have a vested interest in promoting the ideals of radical feminism and homosexuality and abortion. You need to know this fact, because as tomorrow's Christian leaders and parents, you will carry the torch of biblical truth against the destructive errors of popular culture.

Homosexuality and radical feminism comprise an attempt to overthrow God's design for gender. **Therefore philosophic ideals aimed at doing away with the biblical concept of gender constitute spiritual weapons raised up against the knowledge of God (2 Cor 10:3-5).**

3 For though we walk in the flesh, we are not waging war according to the flesh. 4 For the weapons of our warfare are not of the flesh but have divine power to destroy strongholds. 5 We destroy arguments and every lofty opinion raised against the knowledge of God, and take every thought captive to obey Christ. 2 Cor 10:3-5 ESV

As we mentioned earlier, God's design for His creation is expressed in the creation structures He has ordained. These creation structures are often expressed in the form of distinctions. There are at least four sets of divinely ordained distinctions, or differences: 1.) the distinction between Creator and creature, 2.) the distinction between man and woman, 3.) the distinction between human and animal, and, 4.) the distinction between good and evil (right and wrong).

Satan's war against God involves attacking these divinely ordained distinctions. Satan recruits followers by encouraging a denial of distinctions. Satan's hostility toward God first manifested itself in human history when the serpent tempted Eve to deny the primary distinction between Creator and creature. You see, Eve would first have to deny the infinite distinction between God and the creature in order to believe the lie told to her by Lucifer.

In our culture, homosexuality and radical feminism constitute a frontal attack on the gender distinctions God has established. Abortion, homosexuality, and radical feminism have their political proponents who are not satisfied with a political correctness, but wish to pass legislation which protects and enshrines sexual perversion and which permits violence to the unborn.

Can you see why this is not merely an ethical battle, **but is a spiritual war against the knowledge of God?** Here's why—**to take aim at God's creation structures** (heterosexual marriage, gender roles, and the sanctity of life) **is to take aim at divinely ordained distinctions.** It is to attack the very moral furniture of the universe (in the name of freedom, unity, progress, fairness, and tolerance). The evil one is clever. **He is recruiting the rising generation to take his side in this spiritual war.** It is estimated now that 70% of Americans under the age of 30 now believe it is discriminatory to suggest that homosexuality is sin.

The Weapon of Re-definition

Our culture is being set up for a massive delusion. To wage war on the distinctions which God has ordained for our good and for His glory **is to wage war on God who is the distinction-maker.** These distinctions are His idea—His design. As these distinctions are blurred and obscured and eroded; mankind pays the price of being further alienated from the knowledge of God. The Almighty Creator becomes even more remote and removed from the choices of everyday life—**He is pushed to the margins of reality as irrelevant.**

No wonder the number one problem of university campuses today is a palpable emptiness among students. **Once the divine distinctions are swept away** by the satanic broom of homosexuality and radical feminism; **there is little to hold back the advancing incursion of pantheistic spirituality.**

Consequently, we are immersed in a culture that tells us to accept the secular humanist definition of gender in the interest of harmony and equality. But the matter of God's plan for gender and sexuality is more than us staying out of trouble by avoiding sexual immorality and sexual perversion. God's divinely ordained distinctions are joined to the glory and knowledge of God. God is honored, loved, communicated, and glorified when the distinctions He has established are taught and lived. **The knowledge and glory of God are advanced when these distinctions are positively sanctioned and when they constitute our approach to real life.**

By contrast, pagan ideas about spirituality suggest that these distinctions are not creation structures, **but are narrow beliefs imposed on society by the church.** Modern rebels state that the divinely ordained distinctions we teach are regressive, discriminatory, backward, and arrogant. (According to Romans chapter one, that sentiment by unbelievers fills the hearts of those under the wrath of God.)

Because God's creation structures form the very 'furniture of the universe'—to defy these creation structures in one's beliefs and lifestyle **is to run head long into a wall of rock.** God's laws are good, wise, and just. They guard love to God and neighbor and they are inseparable from what it means to be truly human.

The distinctions God has made which are so much a part of God's creation structures are a reflection of the very community within the Holy Trinity. Our Triune God is a community of three divine Beings who dwell together in love, deference, respect, communication, hierarchy, and equality. In human relations, it is rare to see these virtues all coexisting together. The distinctions God has made in gender roles are designed in part to communicate the community (relationships) in the Trinity (1 Cor 11:3).

---

[3] *But I want you to understand that the head of every man is Christ, the head of a wife[a] is her husband, and the head of Christ is God. 1 Cor 11:3 ESV*

The Trinity is the foundation of true community, and the foundation of true community in marriage. **The institution of marriage as ordained by God preserves both equality and difference.** When we look around the world at cultures that do not base its social structures upon biblical theism, **we tend not to see equality and difference in marriage.** Societies without biblical theism are most commonly characterized by marriages which exhibit hierarchy without equality.

Another aspect of differences and functions in gender roles is revealed in 1 Corinthians 11:3. This passage also reveals how the differences reflect the connection between the hierarchy in the Trinity and the hierarchy in marriage. Paul indicates that the man is the glory of God and the woman is the glory of man. Thus, **this hierarchy in marriage stresses the difference in honor and authority.** The man images and reflects the glory of God in a different manner than the woman (v. 7) this difference in role is highlighted in vv. 8-12.

The N.T. draws a straight line from creation to spiritual headship (1 Cor 11:1-16). When God's design for male spiritual headship in the home and in the church is rejected, a distortion takes place. This distortion of hierarchy was seen in the Corinthian church when the deviated from gender roles as defined in creation. Paul answers the gender problem in Corinth by affirming that **the principle of subordination and authority pervades the whole universe.** Woman's subordination to man reflects that greater general truth about God's order in the universe. **Christ submitted to the Father in order to redeem us, and we submit to Christ to be saved from certain doom.** If women do not submit to their husbands, society will be disrupted and destroyed.[1]

The women in the church of Corinth were seeking to abolish sexual distinctions; Paul grounds his reproof in the order of creation.[2] By attempting to overthrow what God dictated in creation the women were throwing off the glory that flows from man to the woman. Neo-pagan reasoning concerning gender roles placed the Corinthians in need of instruction by the Apostle Paul. Paul says I would have you know (11:3). **This is a solemn expression concerning God's pattern of headship.** When Paul says, "of every man," it is clear that he does not refer to Christians only but to all men. The fact that non-Christians do not know these things and do not even want to know them does not do away with the truth of the statement. **Paul makes all a question**

of creation. The woman must have a sign of authority on her head – the necessity of her subjection must appear at every moment. **The women of Corinth raised unrest in the church because they violated the ordinance of God's creation.**[3]

Divine Order is grounded in Creation

Paul establishes that God's divine order for gender is grounded in creation. Christ is the head of every man and he is the unseen Lord, thus men do not have a visual token of subjection to Christ put on their heads. Christ is our unseen Lord, thus men do not have a visual token of subjection to Christ put on their heads. **For women it dishonors her head when she puts away the badge of subjection to her head.** Her man is her true honor because in the institution of marriage, honor flows from her husband who is connected to Christ his Head.

The woman is reflective glory as the moon is to the sun (15:41). In the divine order of creation, the woman shines as light derived from man. Not that under grace she does not come in individual contact with God, but even here much of her knowledge is mediately given through man on whom she is naturally dependent ("let them ask their own husbands at home," 14:35). As established in the Genesis narrative, woman's original being is taken out of man—as it were there is a veil or medium placed between her and God in the acknowledgement of this subordination to man in the order of creation. **Man is made immediately by God** (from the dust of the earth), **thus no veil.**[4]

"And God is the Head of Christ" (11:3). Christ's subordination to God the Father is evident in the Son's work as Agent in creation and redemption. If women reject the created order it brings degradation, not liberation. The wife's glory is derived from her husband. Woman is the divinely made ally of man to assist him in fulfilling his role as steward of creation, thus she is glory of man in her complementary role. **For a woman to step outside her role would bring disrepute upon the wisdom**

of God in His perfect design of the created order. God's order includes relations within the Trinity – 11:3.[5]

Did Adam have spiritual headship before the fall into sin? Adam was a type of Christ to Eve, even before the fall. For, Adam was 'prophet' in his proclamation of God's Word, he was 'priest' in his spiritual leadership of his wife, he was 'provider' in his working of the Gardens to bring forth 'bounty', he was 'protector' in his masculine strength and guardianship. Between Christ and man, and between man and woman **there is a community life, or bond, one in the bond is strong, and the other dependent.** Even under the gospel economy the woman preserves her subordinate role to her husband. A man in Christ has no other Head but Christ. When the Christian man uplifts his radiant brow in worship, it is the insignia that he is the king of nature and he has no other Lord in the universe than his invisible Lord of all. **The woman's covering declares her dependence. The woman's physical constitution is a revelation of her Creator's will concerning her.**[6]

Paul states that the order of authority and administration is the divine structure of things. Man is the glory of God because he is subject to and representative of God's authority. Paul argues for man's exercise of authority over the woman due to the order of creation, the purpose of creation (she was created for man's sake), and the source of the woman's creation (v. 8, 9). The women in Corinth had their heads uncovered in church – as part of his argument Paul cites that the angels are sensitive to our conduct because it so directly reflects upon God's honor.[7]

Author Richard Phillips observes that "the foundational message about teaching and the exercise of spiritual authority within the church as a whole is clear: these [leadership] roles are reserved for Christian men. To the degree that men fail to assume these roles gladly and exercise them diligently, **we end up with feminized churches that can quickly become fruitless and unsound because they are not being led as God intended.**" This says about men that they should be serious about their faith so as to equip themselves to serve in church leadership.[8]

Creation and Biblical Gender Roles

Gender differences are drawn from a contrast in created glory. In his own home the father is like a king – he reflects the glory of God because control is in his hands. When a man covers his head, he brings down that preeminence in which God has placed him. [In matters of worship] if he puts himself under the authority of others – he does damage to the honor of Christ. He is under Christ's authority; he exercises his own authority in the oversight of his family. **The glory of Christ is reflected in [executing a] well-constituted order of marriage.**[9]

Man as the origin of the woman's being is thus the explanation of her being. The creation distinction grounded in the Genesis account is to be manifested in the woman being sharply visibly differentiated from the man. Paul's point is that nature (in terms of natural propriety) expects a woman to be covered – to be uncovered is an unnatural act. Paul makes v. 8 the explanation of v. 7 – man was made solely for God's service, woman was made to be a helper to man. She is the glory of man because she finds her fulfillment in serving him; this is her creation role.[10]

Sexual distinction is not done away with in Christ because it has a creation origin. Paul's argument in 11:6, "Let her be shorn!" is based on the following logic concerning the woman's rebellion – **if she flings away her covering while praying or prophesying, let her also fling away the covering provided by nature** (i.e. her hair). Man is not to wear a head covering since he is by original constitution God's image and glory—he is the glory of God because he reflects the Creator's will and power.[11]

Order and subordination pervade the whole universe—it is essential to its being. When the order is disturbed, ruin results. Concerning the image of God, the chief distinction between the sexes is that the man is the image of God's authority; he is invested with dominion. The woman is equally the image of God, but the dominion that Adam bore, as God's representative, was a dominion invested with authority over the earth. Man as the glory of God is especially the divine majesty manifested.

The woman is the glory of man because she is subordinate to man and not appointed to reflect the glory of God as Ruler. She is the glory of man because she reveals what there is of majesty about him.[12]

Paul's Understanding of Glory

Whatever Paul's understanding of "image of God" (Grk., eikou theou) in Gen 1:27, the essential point for his argument is the contrast he sees in glory (Grk., doza) between man and woman; it is on account of this contrast that the different regulations regarding head coverings are based.[13] The man, by virtue of his manner of creation (created immediately from the dust to rule over the works of God's hands), is the glory and image of God. Woman is the image of God and the glory of man. In this context, the word glory is not the essential glory of God— the word glory in 11:3-15 means to honor and magnify one's head. Man's creation says of God -- what a wonderful order of creature God could create from the dust as His final creation, and the very crown of creation (Ps 8). Woman's creation says of God what a beautiful being He could make from a man.[14]

Man uniquely bears God's image as ruler within the sphere of dominion and authority; in that sense he is created to be the glory of God. Woman was made to manifest man's authority and will, just as man was made to manifest God's authority and will. The woman is man's vice regent and the man is God's vice regent. In this gospel age believing men and women have equal access to God, and they will have equal glory in heaven, but in the current age the creation order is in force – woman is the image of God but not directly the glory of God. Her role, as a helpmate corresponding to him, is to submit to the direction of the man to whom God gave divine dominion. The woman's head covering (Grk., exsousia -- "her authority," 11:10) was her right to pray in public because it represents her subordination to man's authority.[15]

Now this is all connected to God's plan for gender because the wise and just laws He has created (including His commandments for gender) **are meant to reflect the knowledge of Himself.** (Note that distinctions preserve the knowledge of God—men don't dress like women, etc.). Therefore, it is vital that the gender specific commands which God has given be obeyed if marriage is to reflect the knowledge of the Lord. Marriage is to mirror relations in the Holy Trinity of equality and difference in roles. Thus, leadership is clearly tied to male gender because the husband is to mirror Christ's servant leadership—in the husband, it is love, authority, meekness in the same person.

Men are created to mirror divine authority not for their own ends, but the for the sake of those they lead and protect—for the spiritual and physical benefit of those in one's care. (To assume leadership for personal gain, ambition, visibility, self-assertion corrupts the office.) Thus it matters very much to God that spiritual truth is communicated in a relational space of gender distinction (within the divinely ordainedained creation structure for gender). For God's truth is not merely a perfect body of data enshrined in heaven, no, God's truth permeates the creation—it is very fabric of reality in which we move, live, exist, and have our being. Now this culture is filled with seductive lies about your gender and sexuality. Let's look at just a couple of them in order to heighten our level of discernment.

CONCLUSION:

Genesis lays forth a pattern for male and female relations. The arguments for gender roles found in Genesis constitute a loving and all-wise divine plan. The 'blueprint' for the marriage relationship is not only for our fulfillment, but also for the order and glory which brings honor to God. As our culture labors to undermine God's gracious pattern for male and female, it behooves Christians to deepen their grasp and appreciation for God's glorious vision for male and female. Only in this way will we be able to model obedience before the watching world, and before our children.

The gender roles are built into the male-female binary created by God. They are not an imposition by the church. Genesis makes it abundantly clear that the gender roles are a sovereign act of God. For our Creator has given us a perfect picture of gender roles in the unique way that Adam and Eve were created. The Apostle Paul brings the relevance of the Genesis account into the present by imbuing upon us that the gender roles have a solid theological basis. This foundation for the roles is found especially in the uniqueness of Eve's creation: her order of creation (after Adam), her purpose of creation (to be his helpmate), and her source of creation (Adam's body).

Therefore it should not surprise us that Paul develops an all-wise hierarchy of glory and authority. Like water flowing down a staircase, glory flows from God the Father to the Son to the man to the woman (1 Cor 11:3). Headship is about the path of glory flowing through authority. Glory flows from the one in authority.

As we submit to the one over us, glory flows to us. What the world decries as inequality is actually a plan for fulfillment. Our submission to Christ and a wife's submission to her husband is not a mechanical or perfunctory act. To submit to the one who holds us in his heart of love is to find glory and purpose in our relationship. The wisdom of this plan is that our gender roles in marriage are meant to image the very glory and hierarchy in the Holy Trinity itself.

REVIEW QUESTIONS:

1. Romans chapters one and two teach that man has direct knowledge of God's character (Rom 1:18-23) as well as knowledge of a transcendent moral order. Explain what is meant by the statement that 'the work of the law is written in their hearts' (Rom 2:14-15).
2. Why is the nature of truth inseparable from a truth standard?
3. Explain why biblical morality reflects the purpose for which we are created.
4. Explain why pornography 'teaches' a particular worldview of the body?
5. What does it mean: "sex is a whole person activity?" (HINT: a man's character, spirituality, affections, etc.)
6. Why are biblical norms for sexuality inseparable from the nature of reality?
7. Why are acts which dishonor the body dishonoring to God?
8. When the two become 'one flesh' there is a celebration of gender differences which continues throughout married life. Why does this 'oneness' produce deep unity while at the same time maintaining the gender differences of the spouses? (Hint: why are masculinity and femininity heightened in a healthy marriage?)
9. Why does our concept of God and what we worship determine our sexuality?

Endnotes:

1 John MacArthur, New Testament Commentary on 1 Corinthians, pp. 251-263

2 Jamieson, Fausset, and Brown, Commentary on the Whole Bible, Zondervan, p. 1211

3 F. W. Grosheide, The First Epistle to the Corinthians, pp. 247-260

4 Jamieson, Fausset, and Brown, p. 1212

5 David K. Lowery, Bible Knowledge Commentary, p. 529

6 Frederic Louis Godet, Commentary on 1 Corinthians, pp. 535-543

7 W. Harold Mare, NIV Commentary, pp. 637-638

8 Richard D. Phillips, The Masculine Mandate, p. 133

9 Calvin's Commentary, p. 229-234

10 C. K. Barrett, 1 Corinthians, pp. 252-253

11 A. T. Robertson and Alfred Plummer, 1 Corinthians, pp. 229-232

12 Charles Hodge, 1 & II Corinthians, pp. 205-212

13 M. D. Hooker, "Authority on Her Head," NTS, 10:410-416, 1963, 64

14 Grosheide, p.255

15 MacArthur, pp.254-257

Section 4

Male and Female Renewed in Christ

Section Objectives

1. To develop an awareness that the winds of popular culture are 'blowing' against God's plan for family and gender roles.

2. To realize that gender roles of masculinity and femininity are vital to God's glorious vision for relationships which honor Him.

3. To grasp the fact that our natural fleshly defense mechanisms can interfere with the development of godly masculinity and femininity.

4. To learn how the essentials of edifying communication operate as we encourage one another according to gender differences.

Introduction

Two events in the past century have dramatically changed the gender roles in America. The first major change was the **industrial revolution**, followed by the equally revolutionary invention of **the birth control pill**. The change from an agrarian (farming) to an industrial based economy furthermore left its impact upon the gender and family roles.

Industrialization took fathers out of the farm and the shop and brought them into urban centers. The mentoring of sons by their fathers in the skills of the family trade became less and less common. Fathers commuted to the office and the factory and the son was **no longer the apprentice to his father**. Sons began to spend more time with their mothers and less with their dads. The masculine identity of sons suffered as a result.

The birth control pill also changed the face of America forever. Women 'took control of their bodies' by means of oral contraception. Suddenly, the work place had millions of additional workers. Two income families **became the norm**, further **eroding the distinction between the roles.**

Sex without consequences became a part of women's liberation. Women had new 'power' over their bodies and sexuality. Without the moral boundaries of Scripture in place, the pill 'legitimized' fornication.

The watchword phrase of the era became sexual equality. It appeared that women had gained the 'ability' to live as wanton and promiscuously as they wished. They could become 'equal' in in sexual sin; like immoral men, they could be sexually precocious 'without consequence or commitment.'

Hidden inside this Trojan horse of equality was the agenda of humanism. Secular humanism was aware that its new absolutes of political correctness were best furthered in the secular classroom and the media, not in the nuclear family. The Christian worldview of family and human sexuality was viewed as antithetical to the social engineering favored by the humanists. Humanism rejected the biblical truth that society is made up of father-led family units. [1]

By contrast, those who oppose abortion hold to a *holistic view* of human nature—viewing it as **an integrated unity** (the body having intrinsic worth and dignity). Those in favor of abortion are attacking the basis for the value of life—for pro-choice is exclusive: some people measure up and some don't (they are terminated in the womb—not qualifying for the rights of personhood). By contrast, pro-life is *inclusive:* if you are a member of the human race, you are in; you have the dignity and status of a full member of the moral community. Pearcey makes a strong point that terms like inclusive and *holistic* help us penetrate the rhetoric of humanism by pointing out the dehumanizing implications of secular/dualistic worldview.

She also notes that **the divine purpose for male and female is signaled by covenants which nurture life** (and new life) **and affirm design** (teleology). Thus biblical morality reflects the very purpose for which we were created. "Destructive hook-up culture comes out of the culture **of famine for meaning and teleology.**" Hook-up culture (driven by **a secular view of human nature**) is the logical lifestyle implication of young people who are taught that sexual relationships are solely physical, **disconnected** from **mind and emotions**. [2]

Moral common sense is at an all-time low today. Two generations ago it was universally understood that a single woman's moral authority was **inseparable** from her chastity. But, in contemporary Western culture, sexuality has been split from self-hood—the body is regarded **as a piece of matte**r that can be stimulated for pleasure with no moral significance; a neutral piece of matter that can be **manipulated** for whatever purposes self may impose. [3]

Under the tutelage of the humanists, it became incorrect to emphasize the differences in gender roles. Along with set or fixed gender roles, even chastity was considered **a hangover from the age of Christian family values.** Since the sexual revolution, gender equality has been associated with 'sameness'—even in the area of casual, no-consequence sexual behavior.

Not only is this humanistic worldview unleashing a flood of sexual immorality, it is also has the traditional family in its sights. For, according to humanism, **society can only be restructured** and liberated when the traditional biblical building blocks of society (father-led families) are viewed as **repressive and passé**.

In the interest of 'progress and freedom,' the individual's autonomy and place in society eclipsed the biblical concept of the nuclear family led by a godly masculine father.

Humanism's manifesto became a key factor in shaping American society and politics. Gender roles are rapidly disappearing in government, in the workplace, in education, in religion, and in the home. Sixty years ago, a society composed of father-led families was universally accepted. Today every aberration imaginable Falls under the category of normal or acceptable.

The context in which gender roles are clearly visible and distinct is rapidly shrinking. If that context is not the evangelical church and its families, then where is that context to be found? In our culture, adults are told that **gender roles** and generalizations about gender **constitute discrimination**. In schools, in the workplace, in politics, and in social gatherings political correctness tends to flatten out the differences in sex roles. This places an added degree of awkwardness and pressure upon the Christian single adult. It especially introduces an element of confusion and ambiguity for Christian singles in the workplace and in social settings.

There is a need for the renewal of gender roles in the body of Christ. Scripture upholds the gender roles that humanism is seeking to erase. Due to the effects of Adam's Fall, the whole person, along with gender roles, **need to be renewed in Christ** (Col. 3:10).

---

[10] *and have put on the new self, which is being renewed in knowledge after the image of its creator. Col 3:10 ESV*

Our sexuality is derived from God. Mankind is a *biunity*. Our biunity reflects God's image in the most complete form— namely **male and female in relationship comprising a unique completeness** (1 Cor. 11:11-12; Gen. 2:18). The male alone is not the full expression of the image of God. Man was made to be in relationship (even celibate men function best in committed relationships).

Born again men and women submit to the headship of Christ **by submitting to His Word**. In Christ, gender roles are 'renewed' because the Holy Spirit gives the power, inclination, and understanding to follow the standard set by Scripture. God gives the power to follow a different standard than the one set by the world and the flesh. The godly man seeks to glorify God by occupying and promoting the vision for scriptural manhood and womanhood.

In order to be a blessing to the opposite sex, gender roles and gender differences ought to be taken into consideration. **God has made male and female different emotionally,** not just physiologically. Because of that fact, it Falls short of God's ideal for men to relate to women as 'one of the guys,' or for women to relate to men as 'part of the girl's clique.' (Don't try to make it the socializing of 'neuters.')

Even in social situations, men and women need to treat the opposite sex slightly different than the same sex. God has made men and women with differing needs. This is vital to the edification that accompanies genuine fellowship. [4] As we will see in a moment, our Creator has made us complex beings which have a combination of both strong and sensitive elements.

Attributes of Masculinity

Absolute masculinity or femininity seldom makes for a *balanced* person. God has created men to have a soft side and women to have a strong side. The balance involves a masculinity with feminine overtones and a femininity with masculine overtones.

Absolute masculinity and femininity can be viewed as follows:	
Male	**Female**
Initiative	Responsive
Aggression	Smoothness
Rhythm	Melody

But, as a result of the Fall, people tend toward an imbalance of traits apart from the Holy Spirit's empowerment. A healthy balance in a man appears when the steel traits are complemented by velvet traits.

Masculinity (Man of Steel and Velvet)	
Steel	**Velvet**
Leading	with humility
Building	with understanding
Protecting	with attentiveness
Initiating	with gentleness

When it is only the 'steel' traits that a man possesses, he will tend to be a dominant imperious dictator. When he exhibits solely the velvet traits, he will be a milquetoast, unable to command. **Male passivity is the most common distortion of the balance. When the steel is minor and the velvet is *major*, the balance is perverted.** The healthiest relationship and balance between steel and velvet are as follows – STEEL: the majority of the traits will Fall into the steel range, VELVET: the minority of the traits will be in the velvet category.

Attributes of Femininity

When a woman possesses the **liquid traits only**, she will tend to be smothering, self-effacing and **over dependent**. When she manifests the **diamond traits only**, she will tend to be **dominant**, emasculating, and **manipulative**.

Femininity (Woman of Liquid and Diamond)	
Liquid	**Diamond**
Following	with determination
Nurturing	with patience
Trusting	with fearlessness
Responding	with energy

Diamond-only is seen in the character of 'mother knows best' or the 'battle-ax.' A common perversion of the traits occurs when the diamond traits occupy most of the ratio. The proper feminine relationship or balance between the traits is as follows – Liquid: the majority of the traits will Fall into the range of liquid, Diamond: the minority of the traits will be in the diamond category.

The redemptive analogy of Ephesians 5:22-23 provides a framework for gender character goals. Christ's love for the Church is a model of male initiation of love. **He seeks, saves, pursues, and wins His bride by love.** Though He is Lord, King, Leader and Initiator, He sets **aside His privileges** so that He may *give* Himself for her. He sets aside personal immediate rights in order to meet the needs of another.

He is *for* the bride. He gives Himself *for* her. He is responsible *for* her.

She is responding *to* Him. She is responsible *to* Him. She submits *to* Him. She grants respect *to* Him. He dies by sacrificing Himself *for* her. She dies by sacrificing her will *for* Him. Thus, Ephesians 5 provides *character* goals for male female courtship (virtue for the woman, godly service for the man, her goal is godliness, she excels in servanthood – see Prov. 31:10-31; 1 Pet. 3:1-6; 1 Tim. 3:10-11; Titus 2:3-5).

Ephesians 5 provides a **pattern** for courtship. The man wins by love. He is the risk-taker, the initiator, the protector, and the spiritual provider.

The analogy provides the **priorities** for marriage that will begin to be manifested in the dating and courtship phase (see above on the roles depicted in *'for' and 'to.'* Even during courtship and dating, the *'redeemable'* woman will manifest an ability to go in the direction of being 'to' the man). The redemptive analogy sets forth an **example** to the watching world. Biblical manhood and womanhood glorifies God. It honors the Word of God (Titus 2:3-5; John 17:23). [5]

---

[23] *I in them and you in me, that they may become perfectly one, so that the world may know that you sent me and loved them even as you loved me. John 17:23 ESV*

A study of the emotional differences between men and women will be of **assistance in furthering communication and understanding.**

Q: What do men value? Men value the rights of others. They value respect, strength, honor, achievement, integrity, ability, brotherhood, heroes.

Q: What do women value? Women value care, empathy, praise, appreciation, tenderness, acceptance, understanding, attention, respect, honor, protection.

Application: In order to edify the opposite sex, these virtues need to be taken into consideration. As men, we cannot look at ourselves in order to determine what Christian sisters need from us. We have to relate to them as fully woman, **not as 'sub-males'** competing in a man's world.

The man's energy center is his sense of competence (ego). Men operate from this position of inner confidence or ego. From this position, they accept a challenge. They are able to respond with, "I can do it with Christ's help," "Let's move out and go for it," "I believe I am the guy for the job."

It is common for women to fail to understand this. They tend to see a man's confidence in his competence as **pride, arrogance and useless 'chest-puffing.'** The truth is that the man with the deflated ego won't accomplish much. He's got to get his 'p.s.i.' back up! Women need to learn to handle the male ego with care, it truly is sacred—it is joined to the dominion mandate found in Genesis 2:26-28. For man to *rule over* everything that God created (the dominion mandate) requires a degree of confidence in order for a man to assume that sizable task.   God is serious when He commands the woman to respect the man. **Women want their feelings handled with the utmost care, but often run roughshod over a man's ego** center with no regard for its sacredness. The answer to that problem is found in the obedience commanded in Ephesians 4:29.

---

²⁹ Let no corrupting talk come out of your mouths, but only such as is good for building up, as fits the occasion, that it may give grace to those who hear. Ephesians 4:29 ESV

Determine to major in edification and encouragement. It costs nothing and leaves a blessing behind.

The woman's energy center is the 'blender of emotion'. This is the main reason that women are sometimes stereotyped as illogical. Their logic pathways aren't identical to a man's. As a generalization, women tend to evaluate life slightly different than men, incorporating more emotional elements. By contrast, men tend to be more cerebral, they lead with the head. **Men more often see truths and issues in black and white** (which fits their God ordained role of providing spiritual and moral leadership). Women run experiences through the blender of emotions and **draw conclusions** as a result. With that evaluating emotional 'blender' turning, they ask, "How does this feel?" They depend heavily upon intuition and emotional discernment. They often come to the same conclusion as man, but arrive there by a different path. In their decisions, love may trump principle. Women have great powers of empathy, compassion and nurture (these are the perfect equipment for their role as wife and mother).

While men at times find emotions to be a nuisance or an embarrassment, women tend to be more comfortable with emotions. They can try on different ones on at will like clothing. It is difficult for a man to understand the phenomenon of a mother and daughter having a good cry together. Men bond together by service in the same organization, by recreation, by discourse in the world of ideas. **Women bond more by entering into the emotions of others.** For women, emotions are the energy center, the sacred area. A woman who is dating a man or considering a date will sooner or later ask herself, *"Is my heart safe with that man, is that man interested in knowing my heart, how would he care for my heart?"*

What are the universal fears of men and women? This is a very important consideration. Men and women spend a great deal of mental and emotional energy defending themselves from these fears. Often elaborate defenses are erected in order to ensure self-protection.

A man's universal fears are as follows: he fears being subjugated by a woman. He fears being weighed in the scales and found wanting. He fears that he will be inadequate in some or all of his roles and responsibilities. **Unless he is filled with the Spirit,** the greatness of his fear **will determine the size of his defense mechanisms.** Don't discount the fact that men have **an**

inner cry for adequacy. When God takes control of a man's life, that man's 'scorecard' is never the same. The things he looked to in the past for adequacy no longer rule his life. False sources of adequacy include boasting, aggression, comparisons, wealth, materialism, popularity and sensuality.

A Christian man's divine sources of adequacy flow from dependency upon the Lord. God is the Author of a man's talents (Ps. 139:15-16; James 1:17; P. 100:3). A man is to place his confidence in the Lord (2 Cor. 3:4-6), and boast in the Lord (Jer. 17:5-8). He is to daily yield his members to the Lord (Rom 6:11-13).

A woman's universal fears center upon the **fear of being an object that is used and/or abused.** They fear being used as a sex object. They fear being treated as a possession that is cared for and then **abandoned either emotionally, physically or both.** They fear being relegated to the position of a housemaid or a servant or a chattel.

Women often feel like they have to 'have it all together.' Fleshly mechanisms offer them the 'ability' to be in charge of their own needs and vulnerabilities. For a woman, looking out for number one often involves getting others to do their bidding.

False sources of security for a woman involve **controlling others**, being **in charge of self-protection**, knowing what's going on at all times and concealing personal weakness. Often when a woman controls her security agenda with an iron fist, she is revealing that she is **too weak to trust.** By her imbalance in the direction of diamond traits, she reveals a secret heart that is fearful of trusting. **Her demand to control can hide her raging insecurities.**

Scripture says that the woman IS the weaker vessel (1 Pet. 3:7). The more she tries to conceal that fact, the less gracious she will be. God delights in a *meek and quiet spirit* (1 Pet. 3:4). Part of the beauty of femininity is **female vulnerability placed in the hands of God.** This is the opposite of the woman who is in charge of her needs, her security, her reception of love and her vulnerabilities. (Note how this is perverted by a culture that gives a woman permission to use her sensuality/sexuality for personal power.)

The woman with the peaceful spirit is able to receive guidance, she is able to trust, she is dependent upon the Lord and therefore able to respond and care for others. She is delivered from the fear of man and is comfortable with the full spectrum of her womanhood. She acknowledges God as her Defender. She takes her fears to Him moment by moment. Nothing touches a married man's heart more than the character quality of a wife who responds in trust, acknowledging God's wise hand upon her husband.

Men and women ought to have a reverence for the fears and energy centers of the other. Many couples 'fight unfairly' by *shooting* at the sacred areas or fears of the other. Shooting at these areas brings maximum hurt. When a woman attacks a man's adequacy, it is exceedingly painful. **When a man attacks a woman's security and lovability is hurts very deeply.** Some people stoop to this behavior in order to manipulate the other person. It dishonors the Lord because it cultivates distrust and opens the door to resentment. The wise and gracious man or woman KNOWS how to bring encouragement to another and how to safeguard the other person's vulnerability. It is difficult to give and receive genuine edification if one is in the full-time business of self-protection. **It short-circuits effective ministry.**

Our relationships must be characterized by pursuing the freedom to edify others (Eph 4:29). The challenge to be constantly edifying in the body of Christ is closely tied to our dependency upon Christ. As we abide in Him, we learn to grow past self-protection. This is a spiritual discipline to be learned as a habit of life—we grow in our ability to edify others as we exercise greater dependency upon the Lord and also by deepening our expectation that He desires to prosper our fellowship.

Practical Suggestions for an Atmosphere of Edification (1 Cor. 13 applied)

1) Be willing to receive a compliment. Avoid the inner response of, "What does this person want from me?" Pay them the respect of assuming the compliment is genuine.

2) Be willing to express appreciation and encouragement. There are countless opportunities to acknowledge faithfulness in others. It is appropriate to be generous in our praise and approbation. An example could be, "Have I ever told you that I appreciate this about you – (integrity, good listener, willing to help others, etc.)" Be willing to compliment aspects of character. Every person can be an encourager.

3) Most people can remember genuine compliments they received years ago.

When we speak about the excellence of another, it affirms their worth and communicates to them that their friendship is valuable. It takes genuine humility to honor another. Conversation often gravitates to the mundane because people have never committed themselves to edification (Heb. 10:24). As a result, social interaction leaves people wondering if the other person is simply tolerating them.

The Scriptures command fervency of love. Our words are certainly the place to start (1 Pet. 1:22).

A major way to communicate care for others is to show genuine enthusiasm for what God is doing in their lives. **Singles are often pleading on the inside for others to take an interest in them.** Offer to pray for another person.

Find out where the other person is serving the Lord and offer to be of some support however small.

Discover the areas where a person has expertise. Within that area of expertise, ask them questions about subjects that are of genuine interest to you.

You will be amazed how the above skills will lift you above self-consciousness. Once these skills become part of your vocabulary of relational graces, you will begin to grow beyond the concern, "Please accept me, please like me, please affirm me."

Realize that we can contribute immeasurably to another's growth **IF** we are committed to minister to them. Build a base of affirmation; then have fun, enjoy loving the brethren. Once this atmosphere exists where one knows that others in the group are committed to building you up, you can relax and be yourself. It also alleviates a host of fears associated with the expectations and potential rejection associated with dating.

Study Questions:

1. Does moving from a secular to a Christian setting during the week affect gender roles?
2. In a Christian setting, will they suddenly become a key factor?
3. Does the acknowledgement of biblically based gender roles only take place within a Christian marriage?
4. Are gender roles to be exhibited in the courtship or dating phase?
5. Is the role of gender an important consideration in the context of Christian fellowship and social gatherings?
6. Is it possible to relate to someone of the opposite sex within God-given gender roles without concerns about romance immediately entering the picture? (Is a date a proposal for marriage? Of course not.)
7. How is it possible to acknowledge differences as male and female in a pure, edifying and honoring way?
8. How can singles of the opposite sex be a blessing to each other in a fellowship (non-dating) context?

Chapter Notes:

1. Our culture is stepping into dangerous territory by seeking to socially 'engineer' relationships. God has a perfect purpose revealed in marriage and gender roles.

2. When, supposedly in the interest of equality, non-believers 'flatten out' the differences between male and female, it assumes that male and female cannot be equal but different.

3. When believers give in to their fears instead of operating by faith, it will tend to compromise their masculinity or femininity. It is exciting to know that a man's trust it the Lord makes him more masculine and a woman's trust in the Lord makes her more feminine.

Endnotes:

1 Nancy Pearcey, *Saving Leonardo*, pp. 62-63

2 Ibid. pp. 62-63

3 Ibid. pp. 64-65

4 Charles Shores, "Male and Female Renewed in Christ," from an audio series, College Avenue Baptist Church, San Diego, CA, 1982

5 Jay Wegter, "Make your Wife Glorious; the Redemptive Ideal in Ephesians 5"

Section 5
God's Gift of Marital Oneness

Section Objectives

1. To understand that the marriage bed was given to us by God in a moral context of covenant, spiritual union, fidelity, and oneness.

2. To realize that when one of God's good gifts are taken out of their moral context, they becomes destructive idols which enslave us.

3. To grasp the fact that in our spiritual warfare against lust, we need to incorporate the battle strategy of '*out-truthing*' the lie—of beating the lie with the truth.

4. To learn how important it is that the excellent things in creation (male, female, marital oneness) are 'glory pointers'—they should direct us to the goodness of our Creator and His plan.

Introduction

Western culture, under the influence of humanism and the atheistic assumptions of modern science, has redefined sex to be viewed as a basic bodily function. The resultant devaluing of our humanity has caused us to regard ourselves as advanced animals, thus, causing sexuality to lose its transcendental character. The tragedy and Fallout from this worldview shift has given the rising generation supposedly 'scientific reasons' for sexual license.

Christian author Tim LaHaye has good reason to prefer the use the term "act of marriage" instead of sex—he regards the term 'act of marriage' to reinforce its biblical role. His argument for his choice of words was drawn from the fact that secularism had removed the *act of marriage* from the marriage covenant and changed it into a mere physical act devoid of spiritual significance. In our workbook, we are seeking to make a compelling case that the word 'sex' (when describing the marriage bed) tends to be highly reductionist—reducing marital affection **to a mere biological function.** Our preferred choice of words, "the act of marriage" or "marital oneness" helps keep the proper context for physical relations in view—a God-ordained moral context of *covenant, spiritual union, and oneness.* Procreation is of course an obvious purpose of sexual relations in marriage, but the pleasure and intimacy in marital affection are intended to produce a **deep abiding bond between husband and wife** (Gen 2:24; 1 Cor 6:16).

Therefore a man shall leave his father and his mother and hold fast to his wife, and they shall become one flesh. Gen 2:24 ESV

The rising generation of Christians needs to think biblically about this subject of sexual oneness—a willingness to think outside the box of culture if you will. That is essential in order to realize that **God's gift of oneness is multi-dimensional**: it is *spiritual* and *covenantal* as well as *pleasurable* and *procreational.* Humanistic propaganda has so effectively sexualized our culture that systematic biblical instruction in this area is the only way to bring our view of marital oneness in line with God's glorious plan. I am convinced that the church today ought to take a very proactive leadership role in redeeming and reclaiming God's gift of marital oneness. Our young people **desperately** need to understand the glorious context in which the marriage bed was given.

The challenge for Christian men today is how to redeem their sexuality for God's glory while living in a culture that worships sex. In countless conversations with my younger Christian brothers, one of the subjects most frequently discussed surrounds the fight for *self-control in the area of sexual purity.* They often ask, "Where do we find the strength to keep saying 'No!' in the face of a flood of sexual temptation?"

Recently I spoke with one staff member of The Master's College where I teach. He said that the male student athletes under his supervision are exhausted spiritually and emotionally from their efforts to fight sexual temptation all week long. This is a somewhat discouraging picture. These young men are like tired swimmers gulping each breath of pure air, barely able to keep their heads above water. It is all too easy to feel this way when we are being constantly hammered with a message from the entertainment industry: *the highest high you can get is to live for sexual pleasure—this is life as it is—don't miss it—life goes around your sexuality—**sexual fulfillment is the measure of your true fulfillment as a person.***

Of course this is the mindset of idolatry: taking something from God's creation and worshipping it, making it the reason for living, and looking to it for ultimate happiness. **Our culture has turned one of God's greatest gifts into an idol** (Col 3:5). And, in so doing, God's gift of marital oneness (which is intended for pleasure and intimacy and for God's glory) is changed into something destructive. In sexual idolatry, the act of marriage has been taken out of its covenant context and made to stand alone as an activity that is divorced from its ultimate design. Teachers of Christian worldview refer to this idolizing of sexuality as 'a false integration point'. In other words, the idol offers the individual integrating wholeness and fulfillment, but is unable to deliver it. This constitutes the *deconstruction* of God's good gift.

Since our society has deconstructed God's gift of sexual oneness by removing it from its God-given sacred

context, the redemption of sexual oneness will necessarily involve re-constructing and recovering God's plan for oneness. In this article our thesis is that the redemption of our sexuality will only take place **if we *reconstruct* what our culture has *deconstructed***—namely God's gift of oneness. This vital activity of reconstruction is also closely tied to the battle for self-control and purity which is so needed by Christian men today.

Authors such as C. S. Lewis and Francis Schaeffer have described the idolizing of some aspect of creation as ***the perversion of a virtue.*** In other words, God's gift of sexual oneness is good and glorious and virtuous within the marriage bond. But, outside of **the marriage covenant, it becomes perverse**; it is the distortion of a good and virtuous gift of God. Fire is a gift that serves mankind in countless ways; from making car engines run, to heating our homes, to cooking our food. **But, take fire out of its proper context and it is a terribly destructive force** that can wipe out forests, produce pain and death, and deform burn victims. So also the gift of sexual oneness is given in a context for proper use, <u>the context of holy matrimony</u>.

Therefore, our premise is that strength against sexual temptation is in part a function of recovering *God's glory story for marital oneness.* As long as we allow mass culture's idolatrous definition of sexuality to dominate our minds, we will be more subject to its deconstructing lies (especially the <u>allure</u> of pornography). The answer is to *'beat the lie with the truth'—to out-truth the lie.* Our fight to redeem our sexuality will be grounded in reconstructing *God's marital glory story for man and woman.* That is our purpose in this chapter to set forth a biblical strategy for winning sexual freedom in Christ.

Because the gift of oneness has been torn from its marriage context, the entertainment media is telling us that **gross immodesty is 'sexy'.** Modesty is the very common sense application of the sanctity of marriage. Our bodies are to be enjoyed visually and physically by our marriage partner. God commands modesty for very good reasons. Men are especially sight oriented. The more we see the woman's body disrobed, the more sexual desire is stimulated. Modesty in dress is more than a bygone fashion trend left over from the Victorian era—**modesty is inseparable from the biblical worldview of sexual fidelity and purity** (1 Pet 3:2-4; 1 Tim 2:9).

Likewise also that women should adorn themselves in respectable apparel, with modesty and self-control, not with braided hair and gold or pearls or costly attire 1 Timothy 2:9 ESV

Modest apparel in a Christian single woman is a statement that her body belongs to God and to the woman's future husband. Modesty in appearance says that the married woman's body (and the view of it) belongs to her husband and not to the gaze of other men. This is absolutely fundamental to the Christian worldview. Christian women committed to modesty in dress are demonstrating love to their Christian brothers by covering their bodies (and thereby preventing the temptation to lust). Modesty, therefore, is an extension of the sacredness of marriage, and the sacredness of the human body (Lev 18:6-18; 20:17-21).

As men we ought to regard the female body as an incredible and wonderful creation of God which speaks of His wisdom and goodness. The creation of our first parents, Adam and Eve, was an act that magnified our Maker. In effect, the creation of Adam demonstrates that God is so majestic and almighty that He could make a man (the crown of creation) from a pile of dust. Likewise, the creation of Eve declares that God is wonderful in that He could make a perfect helpmate for the man by taking the woman from the man's body (from his rib).

The intimate pleasure God designed into the act of marriage is a byproduct of our differences as male and female brought together in complementary oneness. The marital bond is a celebration of our differences as man and woman—**differences which correspond so beautifully that it is a living poem**

(Genesis 2:23-25). Adam composed a 'poem' on the spot when Eve was presented to him:

"The man said,

'This is now bone of my bones,
And flesh of my flesh;
She shall be called Woman,
Because she was taken out of Man.'

"For this reason a man shall leave his father and his mother, and   be joined to his wife; and they shall become one flesh. And the man and his wife were both naked and were not ashamed."[1]

The woman's body is a marvel and wonder. She was originally taken from the man's body, yet her body (her womb) is the source of the generation and perpetuation of the human race. Now every man since Adam is taken from his mother's body (1 Cor. 11:8-12). This mystery of the first woman taken from man and now man having his birth from woman **is the basis for our interdependence and oneness as male and female**. This means that the act of **marriage is infinitely more than a physical act. It is multi-dimensional. It is filled with layers of mystery and emotion—'poetry' so to speak.** Author Gordon Dalbey notes that this 'mystery' of sexual oneness is too deep to figure out. When we try to reduce it to the erotic or physical alone, it's like reaching out to touch a mirage—its wonder evaporates and disappears.[2]

The differences of male and female which make romance exciting are also evident in the difference in roles between men and women. **The proper order (male headship) is not in conflict with equality and mutual dependence** (1 Cor. 11:11-12). Equal but different is the proper conclusion as we survey man and woman as they were first created, with the implicit recognition of man's headship since *the woman was created for the man.* Submitting to God's purpose, they enjoyed harmony. In the church—as elsewhere—men and women need each other. God intends them to be complementary in their gifts and personalities. Some gifts and aspects of personality may be the same in the man and in the woman, but not all. They were created to be different, and to celebrate those differences to the glory of God.

Our being 'in Christ' does not alter the original order God established for creation and for relationships between the sexes. Rather, our being 'in Christ' should mean that we are better equipped to fulfill God's original purpose in these relationships since from the outset they were 'very good' (Gen.1:31). **When men behave properly, they submit themselves to Christ and His Headship, and they love their wives sacrificially** (1 Cor. 11:3; Eph 5:25-30). Women do so when they behave properly, submitting themselves to their husband's headship. [3]

"Woman is the glory of man" (1 Cor. 11:7). However, He does not also say, "*the image* of the man." For the sexes differ; moreover, the woman is created in *the image of God* as well as the man, but her glory differs from the man (Gen. 1:26-27). Just as the moon bears a certain relation to the sun, so also, the woman shines not so much with light direct from God as with light derived from man (Gen. 37:9).

Then he dreamed another dream and told it to his brothers and said, "Behold, I have dreamed another dream. Behold, the sun, the moon, and eleven stars were bowing down to me." Gen 37:9 ESV

That is, it shines *in her order in creation*—like the moon, she emanates reflected glory—her highest glory is in completing her man and serving as his perfect helpmate.

Not that she does not *in grace* come individually into *direct communion* with God—she does, **but even here much of her knowledge is, by mediation, given her through man, on whom she is naturally dependent.** As we are seeing, the parallel between marriage and the Church as **the bride of Christ** is truly beautiful (Eph 5:23-32). The Church as the bride is made for Christ and attains to her own true 'glory' when she fulfills that end of communing with, loving, and serving Christ, her heavenly

'Bridegroom'. **Thus the Church's knowledge of God and ability to reveal His light, by mediation, is given through Christ the glorified man.** Any departure from this divine order brings 'shame' and 'dishonor' on her (1 Cor. 11:4, 6). The apostle Paul acknowledges that these are wonderfully profound truths which encompass a 'great mystery' (Eph 5:32), but they are given for our joy, wisdom, fulfillment, and enrichment.

32This mystery is profound, and I am saying that it refers to Christ and the church. Eph 5:32 ESV

Our point belabored here is that in the created order, **the woman has poetic elements which declare her creational identity and her relation to the man.** This means that as Bible-believing men, we ought to consider the woman's unique features as pointing to the gloriousness of God's plan. This kind of thinking is an aid to our battle for purity. For, rather than merely thinking of the woman's body as highly desirable but forbidden fruit, **we ought to see her beauty as a collection of *'glory pointers'*.** Namely that her beauty is a masterful composite of elements intended to complement the man (by showing her relation to man). Her design by God is the glorious and generous plan of our Creator to complete the man in marriage, to even be the *glory of man*. This is a cause for great praise and honor to God.

Just to name a few of *these glory pointers*: ever wondered why long hair looks wonderful and feminine on a woman; but a little odd on a man? The answer is that her long hair is given to her by God as a covering, a natural 'veil' which says: **woman was created to need the covering of her husband's care, provision, authority** (1 Cor 11:3-16).

Man's body, by comparison to a woman's anatomy, is muscular, angular, and rugged. This fits his cultural calling as subduer of the earth. Woman's body by comparison is made up of soft curves. This fits her cultural calling as giver of life; nurturer of relationships. These *glory pointers* ought to remind us as men of God's incredible generosity in fashioning woman to be the perfect helpmate for us. These differences are to be celebrated as we give glory to God for making us different.

It requires mental discipline to think in this manner, to think through the 'lens' of God's glory story. But, meditating on the truth in this way is essential if we are to reconstruct God's glorious plan for man and woman. God's glory story is so lofty it requires the Holy Spirit's assistance for us to wrap our minds around what is depicted spiritually by Christian marriage. **The husband is a type of Christ, and the wife a type of the church.**

The propagation of the Church from Christ, as that of Eve from Adam, is the foundation of *the spiritual marriage*. The natural marriage, wherein "a man leaves father and mother and is joined unto his wife," is not the principal thing meant here in Ephesians chapter five, **but the spiritual marriage represented by it, and on which it rests, whereby Christ left the Father's bosom to woo to Himself the Church out of a lost world** (Lu 2:48, 49; 8:19–21). He shall again leave His Father's abode to consummate the union (Mt 25:1–10; Rev 19:7).

"The two shall be one flesh" (Eph. 5:31). In natural marriage, husband and wife merge to combine the complementary elements into *'one perfect human being'*; the one being incomplete without the other. So Christ, as God-man, pleased to make the Church, as the body, a necessary adjunct, Himself, the Head. He is the archetype of the Church, from whom and according to whom, as the pattern, she is formed. This is truly marvelous: the glorious plan of God is to form a new redeemed humanity around the Person of Christ. **We are 'complete in Him'—we are being made fit for God in Him** (Col 2:10). He is her Head, as the husband is of the wife (Rom. 6:5; 1 Cor. 11:3; 15:45). Christ will never allow any power to sever Himself and His bride (Mt. 19:6; Jn. 10:28, 29; 13:1).

And you have been filled in him, who is the head of all rule and authority. Col 2:10 ESV

"This mystery is a great one" (Eph. 5:32). This is a challenging truth to comprehend, but we must grow in our understanding of this deep mystery. This **profound truth, beyond man's power of discovering, but now revealed**, namely, of the spiritual union of Christ and the Church, represented by the marriage union, is a great one, of deep importance. So the word "mystery" is used of a divine truth not to be discovered save by revelation of God (Rom. 11:25; 1 Cor. 15:51). 4

In light of these glorious truths, **it is vital that we take our God-given yearning for intimacy to the holy institution of marriage and not to sexual lust and dissipation (i.e. porn).** Now God has planted in us as men a very strong desire for a woman. And, clarification is necessary at this juncture, for strong desire for a wife is possible without committing sexual lust. **Sexual lust is not the same thing as desiring to be sexually one with a woman.** That desire is God-given and it plays a part in leading a man to commit himself to the marriage bond. By contrast, lust begins by looking upon a woman and fantasizing about making her one's object of sexual pleasure. Lust says, "If I could have her sexually, and not be discovered, I would do so. But if I cannot have her in my bedchamber, I will have her in my mind—in my fantasies." The latter is what takes place during porn use. God hates sexual lust because it is living for pleasure by using a person and **does not stem from God-honoring love and self-control (which are essential to the fruit of the Spirit).**

The answer to our problem of sexual temptation requires a biblical strategy; we need to always be about the business of elevating the truth of God so that we see its beauty and virtue and wisdom. Then, like a great spot light, God's truth will expose the world's lies about immoral sexual indulgence (Eph 5:7-12). Thus one of the great benefits of this strategy is that by feeding upon the **magnificence of God's plan** for man and woman, **a Christian young man will find added strength in building a protective perimeter around his heart affections.** By deepening our wonder at God's glorious plan for marital oneness, our fascination with its counterfeit (lust and pornography) will lose its allure.

Pornography is a worldview about sexuality that wages war on God's plan for sexual oneness. We know from Scripture that the act of viewing these images has a corrupting effect upon a man. Porn functions like a ball of rat poison coated in sugar. The porn user attempts to lick off the sugar coating without coming in contact with the poison—an impossible task because the temporary pleasure surge IS the poison. Here's the reason why: porn cuts new pathways in the brain.

By repeated use, porn 'welds' new 'wiring' in the mind. These new destructive illicit pleasure pathways are reinforced by adrenaline and temporal excitement. What begins as a 'hair-thin' wire pathway can grow into a thick 'cable' through habitual use. This 'pleasure pathway' concept is an inseparable aspect of porn's highly addictive nature. The new brain pathways are directed at eroticized, self-focused pleasure. In that sense we could refer to a 'porn session' as *a tutorial in selfishness—a tutorial in greed.*

Repeated porn use has a killing effect upon a man's potential to unselfishly pleasure his wife. The reason for this is that sacrificial love to one's wife has *redeemed sexuality* at its center. In other words, a man's libido, or sexual desire, when redeemed and placed under Christ's control, is the necessary character trait of the godly husband who will sacrificially put his wife's pleasure above his own. **John Piper says that if we are not satisfying our wife in the marital relationship, we are using her as a mannequin for masturbation.**

Habitual porn use, over time, actually **reduces a man's ability to fully enjoy the marriage bed.** Porn clearly erodes the level of satisfaction God intended in marital bliss. Why? Because porn cultivates **unrealistic sexual expectations**, it eroticizes lovemaking entirely (overshadowing the love and emotional elements), it engenders the worship of youth and bodily perfection, it produces **a distorted view of the woman's needs**, and it 'schools' a man in instant, impatient self-gratification. **It**

trains his heart in selfishness. Rather than wanting to love and serve others he asks, "What can this woman do for me and my desires and pleasures?"

Porn use is causing a crisis in masculinity by making men passive. For the user of porn does NOT have to demonstrate any of the following masculine behaviors. He does not have to: *pursue; win; serve; lead; risk; give himself; conquer by love; communicate; or initiate.* The porn user just passively receives —he functions as a detached user who goes deeper into self rather than being drawn out of self toward another. **Porn use not only** *reveals* **a crisis in masculinity, it also** *deepens* **the masculine crisis.** The man involved in porn is allowing himself to be controlled by lust and is abandoning his godly roles of servant leader while the very male virtues exercised in **oneness are eroded in the process.**

The cultivation of sexual lust through images is a radical distortion of the God-given yearning for intimacy. By reducing sexual oneness to the erotic, porn is the most extensive and convincing mirage in existence. It promises fulfillment, but stands zero chance of producing oneness with another person. This is the reason why the man is left feeling guilty and shameful and self-hating. He is drawn to the 'cosmic glue' that makes two into one, **but there is no one else there.** There is no other person, just himself and an electronic harlot made up of pixels. No wonder he feels ashamed, empty, and hollowed out.

He is attempting to drink from a well reserved for making two into one. He is rejecting the purpose for the gift of oneness. And, in the process, he is temporarily abdicating any possibility of being *a leader, a protector, a provider, a man of character, or a spiritual head.* By trying to have pleasure without any of his masculine roles in action, he is 'sniffing the cosmic glue' without experiencing a speck of its intended benefits (i.e. oneness). In porn there is only self focus, thus a man's sexuality is not being used for God's gift of oneness, intimacy, and bonding. Is it any wonder that long after the porn session, it continues to kick out the Fallout of **shame, guilt, hollowness, pollution, and weakness.**

This is why porn is such a mirage—**it is hopeless and powerless to deliver oneness and intimacy.** It's like crawling up to a desert mirage; in an attempt to slake one's thirst, the person fills his mouth with burning hot sand and gravel.

Thus a major part of our task as godly men is to reconstruct our understanding of God's gift of oneness. We need to comprehend that **the marriage bed is actually one of the means of our sanctification.** Here's why: the husband, *by patience, service, gentleness, sensitivity, leadership, risk and communication, keeps winning his wife's love and trust.* Her response is surrender—she gladly gives herself. The whole man (all the virtues mentioned above) is brought to the marriage bed. His vision is for oneness (spiritual, emotional, and sexual oneness). He reaches the height of his pleasure potential by self-control, patience, nurture, and servant leadership. **She reaches her pleasure potential by giving herself in trust and surrender.** In the process for a Christian couple, their sanctification is advanced; **his masculinity and her femininity are both deepened.** He shows himself Christ-like and she is made glorious. Heterosexual monogamous marriage is the greatest culture making force on the face of the earth because a man's passions are subdued and brought under control for the purpose of fulfilling God's gift of oneness.

As a servant leader, he will find his greatest satisfaction in living as a channel of Christ's love to his wife. The man is 'watered by watering'—he is fulfilled in fulfilling his wife. Porn is the exact opposite—it cannot rise above the selfishness of self-focus and self-indulgence. This is the paradox involved in our satisfaction as men. The direct pursuit of pleasure, with no servant-leader dimension (as in porn use) **sets up an antithesis against our calling to love God first and foremost, and only to love other things for His sake** (2 Tim. 3:4; 1 Cor 10:31).

Conclusion:

Now lest we become discouraged in our fight for holiness, let us consider afresh our gospel weapons. As Luther said, *"the fiends of sin and guilt are always beating up the believer and assaulting his conscience. How the saint needs to see that Christ was given for his sins."* Renewal by means of the gospel is our constant need. Our growth toward spiritual maturity (and godly manhood) is inseparable from training ourselves in righteousness and discernment. Training is the key.

The man of God is constantly building a case for obedience by reviewing the dividends of God's glorious plan of oneness and benefits that flow from it. And he is constantly building a case against disobedience by deepening his fear of God and reviewing the devastating consequences that issue from sexual rebellion. He forms habits which strengthen his ability to discern good and evil. As in 1 Peter 1:13, which calls men to **"gird [their] minds for action," he can see the danger of temptation at a distance,** BEFORE the particular temptation is able to set an ambush for him. This training characterizes the thought life of the man of God.

As one of my professors said in seminary, "When I find my thoughts sliding down into the crude and the sensual, I 'counsel myself' saying, 'higher thoughts, higher thoughts!'" For the man of God those higher thoughts must be God's glorious plan for marital oneness. Higher thoughts involve redeeming our sexuality by returning it to the context of God's marvelous plan for man and woman. Sexual freedom in Christ fits us for the most important relationship on earth, holy matrimony.

Chapter Review Questions:

1. We live in a society that idolized sexual relations. Explain why it is so important to study God's plan for marital oneness.
2. If we allow mass culture's idolatrous definition of sexuality to dominate our minds, we will be more subject to its deconstructing lies. What is our most important strategy against this problem?
3. Why is the act of marriage infinitely more than merely a physical act?
4. Explain what the Apostle Paul means when he says in 1 Corinthians chapter eleven that "woman is the glory of man."

Chapter Notes:

1. Porn use is a lying worldview about sexual oneness; about the body; and about the image of God.
2. God has built into the creation the principle of delayed gratification. When pleasure is pursued directly for self, it is very often sin, lust, and sensuality.
3. The longing to be one flesh with the opposite sex is a God-given desire when it is not turned into lustful activity. When we give that desire to God to allow Him to fulfill it in marriage, we are 'redeeming our sexuality' and experiencing sexual freedom in Christ.
4. Heterosexual marriage is a powerful 'culture-making force' because it demands that a man develop the character necessary to be a faithful father and a devoted husband.

Endnotes:

[1] *New American Standard Bible: 1995 update.* 1995 (Ge 2:23–25). LaHabra, CA: The Lockman Foundation.

[2] Gordon Dalbey, "Healing the Masculine Soul" a lecture at Phyllis Place Assembly of God, San Diego, 1986.

[3] Derek Prime, *Opening up 1 Corinthians*, Leominister:Day One Publications, 2005, pp. 96-99.

[4] Jamieson, R., Fausset, A. R., Fausset, A. R., Brown, D., & Brown, D. (1997). *A commentary, critical and explanatory, on the Old and New Testaments* (Eph 5:30–32). Oak Harbor, WA: Logos Research Systems, Inc.

Section 6

Manhood of the First and the Last Adam

Section Objectives

1. The world's pursuit of masculine adequacy rejects dependency upon God.

2. The cross of Christ is offensive and 'scandalous' to man's natural understanding.

3. The cross is both the judgment of man's ruin, and the escape and restoration from man's ruin in Adam.

4. The manhood of Christ is our masculine model and ideal, for godly manhood is only realized as we live in utter dependency upon the Lord.

5. Our adequacy and fruitfulness as men comes from the ministry of the Spirit.

Introduction

In this chapter we will examine the contrast between Adamic and Christo-centric Masculinity. Adam's "covenant consciousness" concerning his calling meant that all he did in his working and ruling was to be permeated with the awareness of its dedication to God. Adam as *divine image-bearer* understood that

God had crowned him with incomparable dignity. Thus, Adam's identity as divine image-bearer was inseparable from the greatness of his task to reflect God's attributes in all of life's work and undertakings. Author Richard D. Phillips' comments are helpful:

Adam's calling was the calling of mankind as a whole—men and women together—but of males especially. God placed Adam in a leadership role toward Eve, referring to her as Adam's "helper" (Gen 2:18, 20). God made the woman for Adam, and it was Adam who named the woman, as he had named all the other creatures, for Adam was the lord of the garden, serving and representing the Lord his God, who is over all. Adam was not to devote himself, therefore to endless quests for his masculine identity, but he was to be lord and keeper of God's created realm, bringing glory to the Creator as he sought to bear the image of God in servant faithfulness. [1]

Bounty and fruitfulness would result from Adam bringing order to his world. The net increase in the state of order that Adam brought to the creation was to include the raising up of families and communities in which God was loved, honored, revered, worshipped and obeyed. **Adam was to bring *moral order* through the knowledge of God and through the faithful proclamation of His revelation.**

This gain in order would only take place **if the truth of God's revelation governed and permeated every aspect of Adam's life.** Adam's covenant consciousness focused upon his design as vice-regent, he understood that he was God's appointed representative. He was made in God's image, endowed with capacities, and appointed over the works of God's hands, all for the purpose of showing forth the glory of his Maker (Isaiah 43:7). [2]

The adequacy of Adam's unfallen manhood is a kind of masculine ideal. The first exercise of masculine strength on the planet was by Adam, our first father. Adam in paradise was strong, brilliant, tireless, creative, and holy. He tended the garden in an un-cursed world **without exhaustion, perspiration, or resistance**. His work was not opposed by fire, flood, hail, thistle or canker worm. Before the Fall, he did not know failure. Frustration and suffering only came later with the entrance of sin.

In unFallen Adam we see man's unblemished capacity to exercise lordship over the earth as God's image-bearer. Adam's dominion and cultural calling was both physical and spiritual. As a "planetary king," Adam stood as a representative of all of his descendants. As God's appointed *governor* of creation, Adam's obedience or disobedience would affect the *moral* direction of all of his descendants except one.

Adam's conduct under the probationary arrangement in the garden would also affect the direction of the *physical* creation. Because of Adam's sin, the creation was "subjected to futility" (Rom. 8:20). With the entrance of sin came the forfeiture of Adam's effortless kingship. The Fall into sin shattered but did not destroy man's capacity as *divine image-bearer*. As men, our masculinity is related to Adam's manhood, but our masculinity **differs radically** from Adam's pre-Fall experience of dominion. Adam's descendants have a diminished masculinity—their strength has been weakened by the curse.

Adam's Fall into Original Sin

Since the Fall, sinful man seeks to subdue the earth, but not with the glory of God in view. Fallen man labors in an earth judicially cursed by God, thus man faces toil, sweat, and resistance in his labors (Gen. 3:17-19). His power and ability **to carry out the physical aspect of the original Genesis mandate has been reduced, but not cancelled** (Ps 8). Man's work motives have also been altered. The fall changed man's heart—he lost the motivation and sentiment to live for God's glory (Rom. 3:23). Psalm 49 captures the sinner's ego-driven motives that accompany his work (the Psalmist describes man's blindness and dullness in regard to his divine calling: men are "like the beasts that perish" – 49:12).

Fallen man gladly embraces the physical aspects of the creation mandate: "be fruitful, rule, subdue." However small, men have that desire to leave their mark, to make a difference, to carve out an empire. It is a masculine trait **to seek to build something that will be a monument to one's created kingship**. However, man's motivation to work has shifted its focus from the holistic dedication to his Creator to an inordinate preoccupation with the interests of self. Thus, in our natural or carnal state, our labors are shot through **with motives of pride and self-enhancement.**

The desire to subdue the earth remains strong since the Fall, but that desire has been sinfully distorted. Men subdue as a function of their independence from God. They do not dedicate their subduing to the Almighty. They use their subduing to feed their pride of life. **Man's successes are contaminated by the lust of the flesh, the lust of the eyes, and the boastful pride of life** (1 John 2:16). This triad of lusts constitutes the love of the world.

In the post-flood era, the residents of ancient Shinar resisted God's command—they refused to move out of the Tigris-Euphrates Fertile Crescent in order to fill the earth. Their population center was experiencing the benefits of city life. The division of labor in an urban setting meant that food, clothing, and shelter were readily available. Thus, due to the conveniences of city life, the pursuit of the basic needs took up less and less of their time. With goods and services in plentiful supply, discretionary time increased. The need to survive was eclipsed by the craving to build the tower of Babel.

As Scripture indicates, the intent of the builders was, "Let us make for ourselves a name; lest we be scattered abroad over the face of the whole earth" (Gen. 11:4b). Their plan was to make a towering work of their hands the source of their unity and identity, but God 'cancelled' the building project through the confusion of languages. The unfinished tower stood as a monument to their sinful *pride of life.* The tower is like a parable of human arrogance that extends through the ages.

Today, that same spirit of pride manifests itself in a plethora of versions of, "let us make for ourselves a name." In our Fallen world, subduing, building, and ruling are not dedicated to God. The Adamic mandate (evidenced in man's subduing, ruling and building) has been appropriated for the glory of man. Mankind's conquest of the earth is evident in places other than the science lab, the skyscraper, and the farm. And, as we will see in a moment, the sports and entertainment industries also provide an insight into man's nature as a *subduer.*

Man the Competitor

Man as 'subduer' has a penchant for contests. The pastimes of Fallen men have evolved into contests that showcase strength, skill and agility. The sports industry features the *Athlete of the Year, the Cy Young Award,* and hockey's *Stanley Cup,* but it doesn't stop there—the penchant for being the best runs the gamut from pie eating to bass fishing tournaments.

When civilizations no longer had to face the threats of starvation and the Mongol hoards, pastimes took up ever larger chunks of time. In America, when the last cavalry outpost came down, the first baseball stadium went up. Men no longer brought home a four point buck for the next month's venison—meat was placed into cold storage, or today, shrink-wrapped in the store. Instead of stalking his prey in the woods, the husband put on a tie and took the subway to the office.

For the answer to the question "why are we as men so drawn to contests, competitions, and sporting events?" we must look again at the first man. In a single day, **Adam went from planetary king to dying, struggling steward.** Adam's weakened kingship is felt by every man. **We carry Adam's failure in our own persons.** We have inherited his sin and weakness—a 'broken scepter' if you will. From our first father a legacy of Fallen strength has been passed down to us; a scourge of weakness hangs over us. When we consider our desire to subdue, rule and be fruitful, **we are secretly haunted concerning our fitness and**

adequacy for the task. Our universal neurosis as men is, "Shall we be weighed in the scales and found wanting?" **We hate our inadequacies as men. Seeking to compensate, we try to either prove ourselves or avoid risk.**

There is a connection between our *wondering-if-we-measure-up* and our penchant for *measuring ourselves* (2 Cor. 10:12). When we see athletes of our gender who by discipline, training, courage, guts, teamwork, and s2kill excel in their sport, it shores up our deepest fears about male adequacy. We take great vicarious satisfaction in the victories of our city's sports team.

Not only was man created to *subdue and rule over*, he was also created to be an enthusiastic spectator of excellence. Sin has not removed the desire of man to applaud excellence. But sin has ***changed* the object of man's focus in searching for excellence.** When man broke faith with God, his enthusiastic spectatorship went elsewhere. He no longer 'cheered' the God who made the heavens; he worshipped and served the creation and the creature. **Man was created to worship**, and worship he must. He worships every day. If he is not worshipping the One true God, **by default of sin, he will be worshipping and serving the creature and the creation** (Rom. 1:25).

Why do the turnstiles of the stadiums and arenas generate so many billions of dollars per year? Why are these rituals, games and contests such a driving force among men? Why are we so driven to measure ourselves, compete with ourselves, prove ourselves, and rate ourselves? **Why can't men relate without some form of score-keeping?** Why are we so ready to heap adulation on the latest athlete to make the front of a *Cheerios* cereal box?

Created for Wonder, Love and Praise

Man ceased to believe that the knowledge of God was the highest possible glory that he could experience (Jer. 9:23-24). Humans chose to live for the glory of man instead of the glory of God (John 5:44; 12:43). It is abundantly clear in Scripture that the works, wonders, and ways of God are more than sufficient to eternally captivate the heart of man. But, it is only salvation in Christ that can restore man's capacity to glory in God's excellence. The believer tastes only a fraction of what he will in glory. In this life, when the Christian experiences times where he is lost in wonder, love and praise, **it is but a foretaste of what is to come**.

The philosophies of this world promote the denial of Adam's brokenness (Col. 2:8). The whole concept that man may recover his kingship by athleticism, wealth, and influence is not new. It followed closely on the heels of Adam's Fall. From the beginning, sinful man has looked for a "mirror" to reflect back some rays of that unbroken Adamic virility.

Deep within us as men is a veritable lust for the perfect adequacy and masculinity of our ancient first father. Adam's effortless planetary kingship is joined to the masculine ideal of perfect male adequacy. But, Adam's remarkable potential and capacity for planetary kingship is the 'golden fleece' that eludes us. We've inherited a mandate for kingship, but by reason of the Fall, a broken scepter as well.

The natural man searches for reassurances that his case is not terminal. False religion is the great theater for his self-deception. He entertains the optimism that his Adamic wound is not fatal. He comforts himself with the thought that he is not beyond the reach of self-improvement. (In effect, he is embracing a theology that says, "Adam's wound is not my wound, Adam's dereliction is not my dereliction, my deficits can be repaired. **I will prove my adequacy**.") Like the males of the Noah's time, we are still drawn to the "men of renown" (Gen. 4:23-24; 6:4; 10:9).

In Genesis we find the first recorded case of male posturing—of braggadocio (macho boasting)—the first recorded instance of "look out, I'm a bad dude." The defiant speech was given by Lamech in Genesis chapter four.

To my voice, you wives of Lamech, give heed to my speech, for I killed man for wounding me; and a body for striking me; if Cain is avenged sevenfold, then Lamech seventy-seven fold. Genesis 4:23-24

Lamech's words could be taken from a comic book hero or a Hollywood movie. The principle behind it is timeless—**"by an arm of flesh, I shall vindicate myself, vanquish my foes, and be the master of my fate."** Like Lamech of ancient times, modern men choose earthly, demonic ambition and bravado to deal with their dereliction. This is the 'wisdom from below' that comes so natural to us spoken of by James (James 3:13-18). We have our own 'Nimrods' today who receive our esteem. Instead of a bow and a spear with a room full of hunting trophies, they drive red Ferraris. Their deeds of strength are witnessed by hosts of viewers by way of televised instant replays. The hunger of the spectator to applaud excellence generates their 30 million dollar sports contracts.

The principle is the same. **We thrive upon the glory of our heroes; we feed upon the notion of *men of renown.*** They give us the optimism that **we may patch up Adam's broken kingship.** We can bask in the glory of heroes and believe (falsely) that Adam's race is not in a state of ruin. History gives many versions of this theme. The Greeks had their ideal man, orators, philosopher kings, and Olympic athletes with near perfect bodies. The Romans had their military heroes, their gladiatorial victors, and their statues of gods who looked human.

The world's method of proving and recovering Adamic strength is diametrically opposed to God's plan in the cross of Christ. The subduing that has been done since the Fall of man is distorted and perverted by sin. Men build with a view to constructing monuments to their own strength, wealth, and cleverness. It's the hard work done by the arm of flesh that receives the glory. Men want to see Adam's kingship restored by way of a hero—a philosopher king, an Olympiad, or a mighty warrior. We want a hero who reaches down inside, draws upon his power, and overcomes his own weakness.

The impossible Fantasy of possessing perfect Adequacy

This ought to give us fresh insights into our battle for sexual purity. Here is the reason why: **as men we wrestle with our feelings of weakness and inadequacy.** The world offers us a vicarious adequacy through its heroes. My imaginary ideal self is super-adequate! But the Fall of the human race into sin means that my ideal manhood is not going to be reached. Thus, every man faces a kind of crisis in masculinity. The issue is then, how will he handle that crisis?

Within this context of the quest for male adequacy, the devastating effects of pornography reveal an additional consequence. Not only is porn use a misdirection of sexual desire, **it is very frequently a tragic attempt to minister to a personal sense of inadequacy (tragic because it harms our fellowship with God and pushes us further from our masculine calling)**. When I am counseling a man caught up in porn, I frequently ask him if he is experiencing a crisis in his masculinity. God has a better way. Our Heavenly Father bids us to be strong in the strength of Another, in the strength of Christ (Eph. 6:10; 2 Tim. 2:1). In the words of the Apostle Paul, "Not that we are adequate in ourselves to consider anything as coming from ourselves, but our adequacy is from God who also made us adequate as servants of a new covenant, not of the letter, but of the Spirit; for the letter kills, but the Spirit gives life" (2 Cor. 3:5-6).

In understanding this mentality of men clamoring to regain adequacy, we can better comprehend why the cross of Christ is such a scandal to men. The cross is an offense because of its abject weakness. For in the spectacle of the cross, we see a victim perishing in weakness, shame, ignominy, and dereliction. In the cross is the *apparent* triumph of evil over good —pacifism and victimhood in the face of injustice and wickedness. Such ignominy scandalizes the human intellect (1 Cor. 1:18-25).

The eternal Son of God was smitten by the sword of divine justice in the 'room and place' of man. We can no longer doubt that man is vile and deserving of the wrath of God. This lesson the cross teaches us is repulsive to sinners. It offends because it convicts us of our sinfulness and of our *ill desert* (what we deserve). The cross is the proof of human guilt inscribed in blood.[3]

The cross is the great divider of men. Its flames of justice burned against God's beloved Son. Now by that bloody propitiation (atoning sacrifice) God's unbending justice is satisfied, but inextinguishable fury will burn against that man who disowns the substitution of God's Son, and nothing can protect that individual from coming wrath (Heb. 2:1-3; 10:26-31)

The cross, by showing man's ill desert, reveals the human condition. The cross kills our optimism that man can be improved. The perennial 'theology' of our Fallen race is one of human potential. **The cross says the opposite: that we are condemned; that the Fall wrecked our humanity and left it floating like debris on the surface of the ocean.** The cross 'cure' is drastic, for it slays the hope of survival of self. Our natural carnal religious optimism suggests that we have the ability to place our feet on the 'river bottom' of our depravity and walk upstream against the current. We instinctively assume that we must try to do our best and that God will make up for our shortcomings.[4] Scripture tells us **that the law way is a dead end, "the law is not of faith"** (Gal. 3:12).

The cross is not merely unappealing to human wisdom, it is repulsive to carnal natural reason. The Apostle Paul reminded his Corinthian readers that the power of the message of the cross is stipulated upon a proclamation unadorned by human wisdom.

Faithfulness in our preaching means that the *offense* of the cross must be retained in our message (1 Cor. 1:18, 23; 2:4-5). The natural man cannot bear the message that Adam's race is slated for demolition.

The cross of Christ is both the judgment upon Adamic ruin and the means of rescue from ruin. The news is far too humbling that Adam's progeny is beyond repair and renovation. So comprehensive is man's ruin by sin that an entire 're-creation,' or new creation, is the only remedy that can avail (2 Cor. 5:17). The theology of the cross is repulsive to natural wisdom for the very reason that it cancels out the possibility of improvement of the Adamic nature. **The cross condemns the Adamic nature, judges it, calls for its legal prosecution, and slays it at Calvary** (Rom. 6:1-11). The descendants of Adam are yet looking for dynamic leaders who will lift the race to new heights. But in their *looking,* they passed by the Son of God; they crucified the Lord of Glory (1 Cor. 2:8). He was the 'stone' examined by the builders and found unfit to build upon. The builders 'stumbled over' the very One appointed by God to recover Adam's race from ruin (1 Pet. 2:6-8).

Christ intervenes in Man's Dilemma

In the incarnation, Christ assumed a weakened human nature. When the Son of God began His public ministry, there was little about Him that made Him desirable by appearance (Is. 53:2,3). He did not exhibit the stately and mighty physical attributes of a Saul or a Nimrod. In essence, He possessed no more of the Adamic exponents of strength than the average man. Though He was almighty God, He was born under the curse with a weakened human nature capable of exhaustion, suffering, and death. This is part of the paradox of the cross; that the Creator of the universe should come **to earth as a human being physically weaker than unfallen Adam** (2 Cor. 13:4).

⁴ For he was crucified in weakness, but lives by the power of God. For we also are weak in him, but in dealing with you we will live with him by the power of God. 2 Cor 13:4 ESV

But here is God's wisdom towering over the natural man's intellect. Christ's act of submission to His Father, His voluntary obedience unto death, and His willingness to undergo radical weakness and helplessness on Calvary was the appointed means to deliver Adam's race. The thinking of the world is antagonistic to God's way of recovering the descendants of Adam. Sovereign grace is mortifying to Adamic pride. For in God's gracious covenant, Christ assumes the sinner's liabilities and meets the conditions necessary for reconciliation and divine favor. The unbeliever is not ready to be brought so low. For the natural man, the world is a 'playing field' to demonstrate the remnants of Adamic strength.

At that very juncture, **the theology of the cross collides head on with the world's carnal wisdom.** The work of Christ makes it clear that trust in human strength and striving cannot raise man out of his present state of ruin. The N.T. proclamation that "power is perfected in weakness" is anathema to the Adamic nature (2 Cor. 12:9). The cross of Christ stands as a monument to God's justice. It declares that Adam's race deserves to die. The cross admonishes all who dare to deny that Adam's case is terminal.

All that God is now doing is through the Last Adam (Col. 1:15-20). No natural descendant of Adam shall reclaim his kingship by the use of the world. God in Christ has closed up and condemned that avenue. God has installed His Son as eternal King (Ps. 2). Christ is the King of all creation (Col. 1:16-18; Phil. 2:9-11). His pathway to the throne was by way of obedience and submission to the Father. This is the only path to kingship that God recognizes. All that Adam lost, and more, is being restored through Christ's obedience.

But the world is blinded to the truth of the gospel of Christ and to the cosmic implications of Christ's reign as King (2 Cor. 4:1-6). **In their blinded state, the subduing done by sinners is contaminated by demonic ambition** (James 3:14-16). Therefore, it cannot glorify God or advance His kingdom. All of the mighty accomplishments of men will be set ablaze in an instant (2 Pet. 3:10). The subduing that is done under Adam's headship is temporal and 'combustible'. It's motive is too closely tied to the worship of the creature. Only those who own Christ as their King have a restored kingship. Natural men are yet accountable stewards of the earth, but they are not kings in heaven's sight. Only the redeemed comprise a nation of royal priests (Rev. 1:6; 1 Pet. 2:9).

Salvation and Transformation

Christ, as the Last Adam, is making a new order of men and women after His own likeness. Though we labor under the curse and feel our weakness intensely, we who know the Savior are priests and kings before God (Rev. 1:6). **The elect constitute a new race with a new Head. Christ, our "Head," is the Champion who has vanquished Satan and overcome the world.** We as His people participate in the benefits of His mighty conquests. Our chief work now is *kingdom work.* As those called of God, we have a higher priority than clearing brush and taming beasts. We are *seeking first* His kingdom and His righteousness (Matt. 6:33). We are tearing down bastions and fortresses of error and lies. By means of His weapons, we, as His co-laborers, are advancing His kingdom (2 Cor. 10:3-6).

We are building upon the foundation of Christ, the Last Adam. He has appointed us to bear fruit and to have that fruit remain. Only these works which are done under the command of the Last Adam remain unto eternity (1 Cor. 3:6-15). Overcoming has replaced subduing as the first priority of the people of God (1 Jn. 5:4, 5). The first Adam kept the garden and ruled over the works of God's hands. **Through the input of order and nurture,**

Adam encouraged the earth's fruitfulness. Now the people who are the seed of the Last Adam are bringing about spiritual order unto fruitfulness. By taking the light of the gospel into a darkened and sinful world, obedience to God **is displacing the *spiritual disorder*** of ignorance and rebellion. In such a way, the kingdom of God is advanced (Col. 1:12-14).

Everything done by man that is temporary is done in the strength of the first Adam. Everything that is permanent is done in the strength of Christ, the Last Adam. For the redeemed man, both present identity and future destiny are completely wrapped up in the Last Adam. The Christian looks at Christ to see what **his own identity is**. He looks at Christ in order to see *what he is* **becoming**. And he looks at Christ to see **what he will be** (see Heb. 2:9, 10; Rom. 8:29).

---

²⁹ For those whom he foreknew he also predestined to be conformed to the image of his Son, in order that he might be the firstborn among many brothers. Romans 8:29 ESV

Jesus Christ is the Architect of the new man. He is the Author of the new man. God cannot possibly bless us any more than by making us like His Son in holiness and in incorruptibility. It is the height of grace to be made like Christ. It is to be eternally blissful. It is to gain the capacity to enjoy God perfectly. **It is to be mighty in love and power.**

Tearing loose from the remnants of Adamic strength and passions is traumatic. C. S. Lewis likened the process to little soldiers of tin being slowly turned into living breathing entities of flesh and bone. "With every change that comes, that works true life in them, the little soldiers whine and whimper at the pain and discomfort."

The elect of God are predestined unto conformity to the Son of God (Eph. 1:4). Though God has initiated the work of making us like the Son of God in holiness (Phil. 1:6), we are not passive in the process. **God commands us to put on the behaviors of the *new man*** (Col. 3:8ff.; Eph. 4:22ff.).

Christ, the Last Adam is the source of the new man. Christ is the template, the contractor, the goal, and the fashioner of the new man (Col. 3:10). He is the Author and finisher of our faith, but He is also the Forerunner. He paved the way for us so that someday we might be where He is now, dwelling in the very presence of God. In His glorified humanity, **He is the model of what we will be in resurrection holiness and power** (Heb. 6:20; 1 John 3:2; Phil. 3:21).

---

² Beloved, we are God's children now, and what we will be has not yet appeared; but we know that when he appears we shall be like him, because we shall see him as he is. 1 John 3:2 ESV

When we were spiritually dead in the first Adam, we blindly boasted of an adequacy and a completeness that flowed from ourselves. All of this has changed for those who are in the Last Adam. God's work, the work that remains, and God's kingdom work cannot be done with the strength inherent in an arm of flesh. It cannot be accomplished by means of the wisdom with which we were born. The new race, created in Christ, the Last Adam understands that apart from Him, they can "do nothing" (John 15:5). From the context in John 15 it may be asserted that **the believer is utterly dependent upon Christ for the power necessary to bear spiritual fruit.** We can do *nothing* by way of a spiritual work apart from living union with Christ.

In Christ there is an entirely new source of personal adequacy. Those who are of the *first Adam* live to prove their personal adequacy. But, for the new man in Christ, there is a looking away from self as the ultimate source of adequacy. As mentioned earlier, Paul affirms God as the only source of adequacy for kingdom work, utter dependency upon Christ, the Last Adam, is a principle that is in direct conflict with Adamic pride.

Not that we are adequate in ourselves to consider anything as coming from ourselves, but our adequacy is from God, who also made us adequate as servants of a new covenant (2 Cor. 3:5, 6a).

The principle of the death to the Adamic man is the principle of the cross applied. It is a dynamic that is present in all true Christian ministry. Paul declares, *"But we have this treasure in earthen vessels, that the surpassing greatness of the power may be of God and not from ourselves..."* (2 Cor. 4:7).

The Apostle recognized that the pride of man is quick to glory in a person. God, in His wisdom, is able to emphasize the *'earthen'* nature of human flesh in order that all the glory might go to God and not to the messenger. The *'treasure'* (the spiritual life and truth contained in the earthen vessel, God's messenger) is solely from God.

The problem is that men worship and serve the creature and the creation. In so doing they discount the unseen God of all power and instead esteem a sinful man who stands in front of them. We have opportunities to represent God in ways the unsaved do not: glory of God; magnify His grace; love and live and teach His transforming truth.[5]

The cross judges all that we were in Adam in order that Christ may be all in all. The cross is the source of the believer's victory. It severs him from any legal attachment to Adam and it attaches him to Christ in an eternal, living, and fruitful union (Rom. 6:5-9; 7:4). (Paul also attributed his severance from, or 'crucifixion to the world,' to the power of the cross – Gal. 6:14).

In Adam, we were always searching for completeness. Like a man running to and from with a puzzle piece, **we ransacked the world in an effort to find some combination of things that would complete us.** Before we were *'crucified to the world,'* we saw the world as our workshop. We exercised a misinformed optimism **that the world could provide the source of our completeness**. We typified the *'earthy man'* described by Paul in 1 Corinthians 15:47, 48. The *'earthy man'* materialized all of his soul's needs and took them to the offerings of Vanity Fair ('Vanity Fair' was Bunyan's allegorical title in *Pilgrim's Progress* for the lusts of this world).

The new man has completeness by reason of his union with Christ. The Christian has been crucified to the world as a source of completeness, and his completeness is in Christ (Col. 2:10). In Christ the saint is given a restored stewardship that is spiritual now, and someday, in the Messianic age, physical as well (Rev. 2:26; 3:21). **Because of completeness in Christ, the believer will someday participate in the liberation of all of creation from the bondage of corruption** (Rom. 8:18-25).

---

24 For in this hope we were saved. Now hope that is seen is not hope. For who hopes for what he sees? 25 But if we hope for what we do not see, we wait for it with patience. Romans 8:24-25 ESV

The new man is constructed around Christ. He does not have, nor will he ever have, a completeness that is autonomous from Christ. Adamic man makes a futile attempt to find that completeness by looking to himself and to the world. **The new man will never lack completeness.** Paul's logic in 1 Corinthians 15 is flawless: The empty tomb *proves* that our 'Man in heaven' will share His heavenly image with those who are in union with Him. *"And just as we have borne the image of the earthy, we shall also bear the image of the heavenly [man]"* (1 Cor. 15:49). (See Paul's argument in 15:35-46. In establishing proof that there is a resurrection body for believers, Paul appeals to Christ's glorified existence. Christ's resurrection glory followed His mortal existence on earth. The same glorious change awaits believers.) **In this very context, Christ is referred to as the "last Adam." Christ is the "*second man.*" As the last Adam, He is the "*second*" founder of a race of men—spiritual men** (1 Cor. 15:47, 48). These spiritual men, by virtue of their completeness in Christ, will most assuredly bear the image of the Man who came from heaven (15:49, 50).

---

47 The first man was from the earth, a man of dust; the second man is from heaven. 48 As was the man of dust, so also are those who are of the dust, and as is the man of heaven, so also are those who are of heaven. 49 Just as we have borne the image of the man of dust, we shall also bear the image of the man of heaven.1 Cor 15:47-50 ESV

If the cross contains God's verdict concerning the Adamic man, then the empty tomb speaks of God's promise of glory for the new man. The cross puts the destinies of Adamic man and the new man into sharp contrast and bold relief. The man who exercises faith in God's Word apprehends this contrast with ever-increasing clarity.

The godly man understands the times. He sees that we live in a culture that is dead set on making us forget the contrast. Our culture is enamored with what remains of Adam's glory. **Youthfulness, strength and beauty are worshipped in our land.** The media woos the next generation of youth **by selling the promise of Adamic prowess.** From Barbies to Masters of the Universe, it is the gilding of Adamic exponents. Muscle-bound action figures fill the shelves of toy stores. These plastic Nimrods give our **youngsters what they crave; the fantasy of possessing perfect adequacy.** King Saul of ancient Israel was head and shoulders above his countrymen. He was a courageous warrior and a handsome leader. But God brought the people's choice (Saul) into bold contrast with His choice in a king.

David was God's choice. He did not possess the Adamic exponents of Saul, **but David was a man after God's own heart.** Like David, **the new man has a passion for God's glory.** As Christian men, **can we follow Christ as His disciples and be captivated by Adamic exploits at the same time?** If we attempt to do both, **we will cast a cloud over the hope of glory that is to animate our affections. We will fall short of Paul's single focus to answer the upward call** (Phil. 3:14). Let us pursue a united heart and follow the Apostle's example. Paul saw the destiny of the new man so clearly that he did not resent the "tarnishing" of what remained of the Adamic man in him,

---

Therefore we do not lose heart, though our outer man is decaying, yet our inner man is being renewed day by day (2 Cor. 4:16; Rom. 8:10).

This present age assaults us with the Adamic value system—a system that espouses personal adequacy by the use of world. **With that corrupt value system comes the concealment of the fact that the first Adam's act of disobedience inaugurated the reign of sin and death** (Rom. 5:17-21). Let us remember that because of Christ's act of obedience, we have been made righteous, we have been brought into the sphere of abounding grace (Rom. 5:18-20). Our male pride centers around the Adamic man and his capacity. Let us hold fast enough to Christ that we might release that pride and make Paul's formula our own. "*When I am weak* [in myself], *then I am strong* [in Christ]."

Because of the last Adam's act of obedience, we are presently priests and kings 'in training.' The consummation will come about after our brief journey in these mortal bodies. Christ's resurrection is the warranty of the new man's future existence. As we strive to remain upon the narrow path for one more week, let us look up by faith at our Man in glory and contemplate the destiny of the new man (Heb. 2:5-9ff.).

CONCLUSION:

In order that God may receive all of the credit, says Paul, *"[we are] always carrying about in the body the dying of Jesus, that the life of Jesus also may be constantly manifested in our body"* (2 Cor. 4:10). Paul equated the value of his own suffering with the necessity of having *"the life of Jesus manifested in his mortal flesh"* (4:11). What a radical contrast this is from the Adamic tendency to glory in a super-hero. The cross is continually applied to the saved descendant of Adam until death. The cross puts to death what we were in Adam. Paul looked to his 'co-crucifixion' with Christ for the power to subdue sin (Gal. 2:20; 5:24; Rom. 6:6).

Endnotes:

1 Richard D. Phillips, *The Masculine Mandate, God's Calling to Men,* Lake Mary, FL: Reformation Trust, 2010, pp. 7-8

2 For a discussion of Adam's role as *prophet, priest and king,* see the excellent book by G.I. Williamson, *The Westminster Confession of Faith for Study Classes,* P & R Publishing, 1978, pp. 44-45.

3 Gardner Spring, *The Attraction of the Cross,* Banner of Truth, pp. 206-207

4 Gerhard O. Forde, *On being a Theologian of the Cross, Reflections on Luther's Heidelberg Disputation, 1518,* Eerdmans, 1997, p. 18

5 Richard Phillips, *The Masculine Mandate,* p. 33

Section 7
The Glory Story of God in Christ

Section Objectives

1. To learn that there is value even in our disillusionment and discouragement with self. For God is showing us the infinite difference between Christ and self.

2. To understand that God is faithful in His fatherly love to discipline us, for in so doing He opens us up again to be captivated with, and be changed by His glory.

3. To learn that as the Lord applies the cross to us, He is changing us by making us more like Christ.

4. To grasp the truth that God's grace did not add Christ to our life; instead divine grace brought us into God's glory story in Christ.

5. To learn that in Christ our highest possible good has been joined to God's eternal plan to glorify Himself through the salvation of sinners.

The Glory Story of God in Christ

Many Christian men are living in a harness as if the 'yoke of Christ' is heavy and burdensome (Matt 11:30; 1 Jn 5:3). If you think that the commandments of God are *burdensome,* **it shows that you still love the world.** As a consequence, these men live by the rule of the temporal and the tyranny of the urgent without a perspective of the glory of God. Since their lives are bound up in temporal concerns, the *glory story* is far from the horizons of their thought life. They have become enemies of the cross of Christ, controlled by their carnal appetites and consequently have set their minds on earthly temporal things (Phil 3:19).

True Christians are far different from 'worldlings' because God has made them new creations—they have been made complete in Christ—and have a whole new set of values (2 Cor 5:17). The Lord continues to apply the cross to what remains of their carnality, self-centeredness, and indwelling sin. God breaks into the believer's self-obsessed world with massive self-disillusionment. But, what we often fail to see is that this disillusionment with self is critical to our progress in the faith.

Let's consider the source of our disillusionment. **It is our fleshly pride-of-life mode of imagining that we are the sum total of our accomplishments.** This is our default mode. In our pride-of-life reasoning we falsely assume that by our performance, we are the architects of our own glory, security, and honor. Every lapse of faith tends to be a return to this default mode of performance and pride-of-life thinking (1 Jn 2:15-17).

Our Heavenly Father faithfully disciplines us as His sons (Heb 12:4-13). *God breaks into our shrunken truncated 'self-ordered' world by sending losses, crosses, mediocrity, and stagnation.* He catches us in His 'net'—we feel as if our life is in freeze frame mode (Ps 66:11). Try as we may we can't seem to make things happen like we used to. Our real problem is that we fail to discern that God is scraping us down to bedrock. But while in that *freeFall,* it can feel like God is against us and has abandoned us as He methodically kicks out each of the things which support our ego (our 'ego props'). In the midst of this we have little idea that this is for our good and that we will land again on Christ our true foundation, our *continent of rock* (Heb 6:18). The psalmist describes this process: "My flesh and my heart may fail, but God is the strength of my heart and my portion forever" (Ps 73:26).

The Lord has to do this strange work in our lives on a semi-regular basis because we so quickly depart from feeding upon Christ as He is exhibited in the glory story of the gospel. So God breaks into our world, into **our little hut made out of the sticks** of manageable Christianity. He does this in love—applying the cross of Christ to us—for it has been far too long since we have seen His glory. But having our ego props kicked out is a dangerous thing because we can so **easily turn to false sources of comfort.** Self-pity and sensuality may beckon us; or more ego vindicating activities may make overtures to us (offering to restore ego supports and prop up the afflicted self).

It is in these times when God has *caught us in His net* (Ps 66:11ff.) that He sends disillusionment for one great purpose: that we might ponder afresh the infinite difference between self and Christ. The flesh loves *Gnostic Christianity* (with the religious self at the center instead of Christ as He should be—Galatians 2:20, "*not I but Christ*"). In that spurious Gnostic form of religion the vastness of Christ is lost and the infinite difference between Christ and the religious self is obscured. Our part is to submit to His discipline as He deals with us in perfect fatherly wisdom (Heb 12:5-9). Our Heavenly Father's discipline knocks us off center—it decentralizes self. We may lose our balance and become a bit spiritually disoriented in the process, but this is all for the great purpose of conforming us to the image of Christ (Rom 8:28-30).

Paul writes the book of Colossians to restore the supremacy of Christ in the minds of the Colossian believers. They were tempted by an incipient form of Gnosticism (see the 'Christ hymn' found in Colossians 1:15-21 designed to exalt Christ's supremacy). So God allows us to descend into deep self-disillusionment in order to startle us with our weakness, sinfulness, and unfruitfulness. This disillusionment is often with our "religious self"--we become disgusted and disenchanted with our religious performance. As God's servant, our productivity may take quite a hit. The work of service that God has been doing through us may stagnate--we seem to be temporarily 'shelved'.

What we thought was a much needed ministry may dwindle for a time. Our fruit-bearing may see drought.

This disillusionment sends seismic waves through our manageable form of Christianity. We are defining *manageable Christianity* as a Christianity that is blind to the glory of God in Christ. For in manageable Christianity, the saint may go for months without experiencing any awe over the great things of God. **God chooses disillusionment to blast us out of our self-focused narcissistic religious practices.** In order for Christ to assume His proper place of glory in our lives, **the idea that we are the sum total of our accomplishments must be dashed.** God is dealing with our instinctive sentiment that our deeds and misdeeds ultimately define us. We find that the cross of Christ applied to us keeps blocking our hand from burning **incense** to our accomplishments. This is the Lord's 'strange' work of humbling us that He might exalt us.

The Lord is especially diligent to discipline those in Christian ministry. (Rev 3:19; Heb 12:1-12ff; 1 Pet 4:12-13; 5:10; James 3:1). God's servants must be frequently re-calibrated by views of God's glory. In our spiritual ambition we tend to reduce our Christianity down to our Christian service and our devotion to God, thus attempting to solicit His help for our Christian ministry agendas so that our 'fruit production' will be uninterrupted.

As such, the Lord may *freeze* our ministry fruitfulness until we are willing to say, "Lord, show me your glory!" When Moses wanted to quit, it was *show me your glory* that got him back on track amidst the greatest challenges imaginable (Ex 33:18ff). **When we are most obsessed with our ministry and our fruits and works (or lack thereof), we are actually in the poorest position to be fruitful.** That is the great paradox. When most self-obsessed, even in being preoccupied with excellence and production, we may be worlds apart from true fruit-bearing. How different is God's way. His way is the glory way: *we behold His glory; we are transformed by His glory; we then proclaim His glory* (we proclaim His excellencies, 1 Pet 2:9-10). Only the gospel can take us off of self and out of debilitating self-consciousness. We cannot transcend self—self cannot cast out self. The glory story of the cross alone can change us.

In glory-less, manageable Christianity we don't want to feel our utter dependency on the Lord. We want God to come along side our plans, and we forget that He saved us to communicate to us Himself through the **glory story.** In our glory-less state we forget that we need **constant strengthening** in the inner man in order to be able to understand, grasp, and **comprehend God's love and glory in Christ** (Eph 3:16-19). God busts us out of our manageable Christianity by showing us His glory—by drawing us into His glory plot again—instead of leaving us in our own attempts to **draw Him into** our life agendas.

Whole churches, whole movements, whole denominations are so dead set on their religious agendas they are for the most part blind to the glory of God in Christ as the ongoing nourishment of the soul. It makes us wonder aloud how it will go with them at the *bema judgment* (the judgment seat of Christ), for works not founded upon Christ and His glory will be burned up (1 Cor 3:13-15). Like the church of Ephesus in Revelation chapter two, they were so busy for God **and yet they left their first love.** They did not keep repenting over this departure from Christ and they eventually **lost their lamp stand.** They were more interested in production than in communing with Christ and beholding His glory and were more focused on quantifying their works than in bearing fruit that came from abiding in Christ (Jn 15:1-5).

---

[1] *"I am the true vine, and my Father is the vinedresser. [2] Every branch in me that does not bear fruit he takes away, and every branch that does bear fruit he prunes, that it may bear more fruit. [3] Already you are clean because of the word that I have spoken to you. [4] Abide in me, and I in you. As the branch cannot bear fruit by itself, unless it abides in the vine, neither can you, unless you abide in me. [5] I am the vine; you are the branches. Whoever abides in me and I in him, he it is that bears much fruit, for apart from me you can do nothing. Jn 15:1-5*

Stranded on a Desert Island of Performance

Temporal concerns always work to crowd out the sight of God's glory—even temporal concerns in ministry. Human excellence becomes a substitute for the glory of God. Worship teams, hype, emotion, socializing, fanfare, and sentimentality become the dry husks of religion we are eating instead of feeding upon Christ and His glory. What is highly esteemed by man is detestable in the sight of God (Luke 16:15). It makes us wonder why we don't hear a cry in our churches, "No more husks! Show me Christ!"

Now what, where, and **how do we behold the glory of God?** First of all, the glory of God is beheld **in the face of Christ** (2 Cor 3:18-4:6). God moves His glory out of the realm of abstraction and into our experience by showing it to us in Christ. Only there does His glory become perceivable, tangible, and salvific. Still we need strengthening to attain, to comprehend, and to behold that glory so that we might be changed thereby (Eph 1:17-18; 3:16).

As Fallen men we are still drawn to **operate as a *human 'doing'***—drawing our value from all of our accomplishments. But when the grace of the cross applied: *trial, loss, setback, weakness,* and *even confusion* and *disillusionment* become the tools in God's hands **to startle us to see the infinite difference between self and Christ.** Only then do we want God Himself as the solution instead of our beloved agendas. This is the cross applied to our flesh, opening us again to His glory.

Now the divine glory story concerns the covenant of redemption; that God chose a people and gave a bride to Christ. BUT, this bride in her natural state was corrupted, polluted, and without the heavenly virtue of holiness, but even more, she was a rebel, dead in sins and intent on killing Christ, her future husband. At the heart of the **glory story is this plan, a plan so immense in glory** so as to fill eternity. In order for Christ to win, raise, claim, be espoused to, and take His bride, He must assume her liabilities, her moral failure, her pollution and her alienation from God. He must gladly take upon Himself the very things that kept her from Him. He must take on her moral alienation, her wrath, her punishment, her death, and her agony. Only then could He be her righteousness, glory, virtue, life, light, blessedness, love, security, and destiny.

He so radically identified with her condition that He closed the infinite gap between **dead wicked rebel** and self-existent holy God. Our meditation upon glory therefore involves thinking upon this gap that Christ closed in His incarnation and redeeming work —a gap so great that the distance between her tomb and her throne could only be spanned by the willingness o**f the God-man**. Christ, by the immensity of His Person, fills the gap between the innate poverty of His bride and the riches of eternal glory (2 Cor 8:9). He closes the gap between her just deserts and her new destiny. The glory story of God in Christ gives us the glory of God—for the glory of God revealed in the face of Christ is how we have come to know God. God has shown us His glory and Himself in the face of Christ (2 Cor 4:4-6).

But the cost is remarkable (Mk 10:45). Christ had to become a human cadaver carried by sinful men to a stone tomb so that we could be with Him forever in glory. Let this distance that He spanned stagger you. This distance from flawless glory to polluted dust, **from perfect access and belonging in the presence of God to alienation from Him**, this distance spanned by Christ is so amazing that it is a teaching tool to instruct angels in the wisdom of God (Eph 3:9-11). It is the glory of God put on display in our salvation. It is the gloriousness of Christ's Person in assuming the condition of His bride in order to give her His status, His relationship, and His right-relatedness to the triune Godhead. This means that how God saves in Christ (by His taking on of all of our liabilities) has become the primary revealer of the eternal glory of the Godhead.

But it gets even better, for God is allowing us and even commanding us to handle this heavenly treasure and to fix

our minds upon it (Col 3:1-4). In fact, we must handle this treasure if we are to pass through this life without becoming idolaters. Handling this treasure is manna for our souls and food for our hope. We must feed upon Christ and His glory or by default we will not be unscathed by the world. Without this glory we will attempt to feed our eternal souls on the bogus bread of this world.

The glory story is how God has dispelled the ancient lie of Eden from our souls. The darkness in every unbeliever's soul is composed of the remnants of Satan's original lie—that lie consisting of the proposal that our good and God's glory are at odds. The lie drives a wedge in the soul and we collectively as a people, by acting upon the lie, have forfeited our sight of His glory and our desire for His glory (Rom 3:23; 1:22-24ff). Knowing God is our glory, because our glory is a derived, reflected glory. This is why our boast is to be in our knowledge of the glorious One (Jer 9:23-24). Those who reject God's glory, and who consequently worship created things and human wisdom, will lose all their glory the moment they die (1 Cor 1:19; 2:6-8ff.).

So, in review, the ancient lie of Eden suggested that God's glory and our good were hostile to one another. The lie asserted that God's glory was opposed to human potential and thus God's glory should be abandoned in the interest of self-directed self-fulfillment (nothing has really changed!).

Only by the cross of Christ are God's glory and our good rejoined in our thinking and loving (that is, in our affections and desires). Only by the diet of the cross will God's glory and our good stay joined and fused. We cannot function successfully in the world as worshipping children of God without the cross.

The world, the flesh, and the devil all conspire to reassert the lie that God's glory and our good are at odds. It always pushes for the possibility that there is a higher good than God's glory (a glory which includes His moral majesty and laws). The lie always proposes that abandoning oneself to God's glory is risky and not in one's highest interest.

The church is suffering from cultural Christianity because the sight of God's glory is obscured through a 'rationing' of the gospel of Christ (we sometimes refer to this ailment as the gospel gap). Where gospel preaching is in short supply, a gap grows. The Apostle Paul dealt with a similar problem in the Corinthian church. Paul gives the God-ordained solution to the Corinthian catastrophe. It is as simple as it is potent: the cross is the diet of the mature believer. Anything less, and we will find ourselves attracted to the impotent wisdom of man (1 Cor 1:18-25).

God saved us by granting us a sight of His glory in Christ. The moment when by faith we beheld the Son of God dying in our place—pumping out His heart's blood onto the dusty Judean soil for the likes of us—we came to know God through the sight of His reflected glory in our Savior. We no longer regarded His glory and our good to be at odds (Jn 3:14-18).

Christ in our nature and in our place as a suffering substitute removed the darkness placed there by the original lie. When God showed us His glory in the face of Christ, our hearts were flooded with light. The enmity there was cleaned out and replaced with the saving knowledge of God—we became reconciled to the God of the universe (Col 1:21-22). Now God's cause, which is His glory, has become our cause. By the mercies of God we are rationally abandoned to this cause of doing all for His glory (Rom 12:1-2; 1 Cor 10:31).

The church only thrives when the glory of God is displayed to her in the face of Christ. The church will languish without this steady sight of the glory of Christ.

How do we behold His glory? What is the content of this glory beholding? We contemplate His saving work toward us, for in that redemptive work His glory is revealed (note the 'alphabet' of benefits catalogued in Ephesians 1-3 of God glorifying His grace). We study His redemptive work so that we may be able to proclaim His excellencies (how and why He has called us to be His unique people (1 Pet 2). We dwell upon our relationship with the Father as it is perfectly and wonderfully settled in Christ. That becomes the divinely ordained vantage point from which we behold His glory.

We do not study God from a vantage point of theory **but from the perspective that His glory has constructed a perfect refuge for us.** The wonderful excellencies and perfections of God are spelled out most gloriously and understandably in the endlessly wonderful theme of: who is God toward me in Christ? All of these are access points; windows; portholes from which and through which we gaze upon His glory as our blessed vocation, beginning now and continuing eternally in heaven.

REVIEW QUESTIONS:

1. Why does the Father's discipline correct our spiritual blindness and make us more focused on His glory?
2. What are some of the themes connected with the glory of the Lord? (HINT: *consider how far Christ went to deliver us and win us as His own. Think about who your Savior is: Creator, Redeemer, Judge.*)
3. How did Satan' lie make the human race into idolaters?
4. Explain how the 'sight' (by faith) of the glory of God saves us.

Section 8

The Gnostic Disconnect Part 1

Section Objectives

1. To examine why a divided view of life (which separates faith from life) produces a dangerous 'disconnect' between body and soul/spirit.

2. To learn that there are no separate compartments— the body and soul operate together so that our Christianity cuts across all of life.

3. To learn more about the growing error in our culture: that a 'Gnostic' or divided view of reality, opens the door to all kinds of sexual immorality.

4. To understand that true spirituality involves daily presenting one's body as living sacrifice to the Lord.

The Great Disconnect

By *Gnostic disconnect* we mean that people tend to see spirituality as a **set of private convictions rather than comprehensive truth which governs the totality of a person's life**. When the disconnect is present, religion is regarded as a set of private convictions 'disconnected' from the whole person and his entire experience. To live with the disconnect is to NOT see the human body as the primary spiritual resource to serve God and others.

The disconnect is an aberration or distortion, for Paul and Jesus always remind us that out of the heart comes sin. **And, not only does the heart express itself in the deeds of the body, the deeds of the body affect the soul. Therefore, those who say, "Jesus doesn't care what I do with my body as long as I have Him in my heart" are dead wrong.** The premise of this chapter is to help the reader understand that the **greater the disconnection between the spirit and body, the wider the entry point for immorality and pornography**. God expects our body-soul unity to operate as one in our worship and service. As our Redeemer who purchased us and owns us, Christ has the rightful claim to every square foot of our life. There are no separate compartments. The body and soul operate together so that our Christianity cuts across all of life. To be subject to the lordship of Christ is to understand that Christ is Lord of every square inch of our life experience.

Thus, the Christian is dead to sin because he has died with Christ. The outworking our death to sin is to be lived out daily—we are to present ourselves to the Lord each day. Our progress in personal holiness depends upon the daily presenting of our bodies to the Lord. It is this principle of presentation consistently applied which ends the dangerous disconnect.

"Therefore do not let sin reign in your mortal body that you should obey its lusts, and do not go on presenting the members of your body to sin as instruments of unrighteousness; but present yourselves to God as those alive from the dead, and your members as instruments of righteousness to God" (Rom 6:12-13)

Porn & the Disconnect between Faith and Life

A Gnostic-like disconnect is re-emerging in the church today. The attitude of ancient Gnosticism was, *since we have received divine knowledge and are enlightened, it really doesn't matter how we live in our bodies.* Ascetic Gnosticism taught that the physical things of the world were evil and that to attain holiness one must be detached from them. However, antinomian Gnosticism realized this was impossible and taught the false doctrine that God's free grace allows us to live in our body licentiously because the spirit alone is important (as if God's grace has removed the danger of sinning). "Therefore, [according to this view of spirituality] whatever one does in the body doesn't matter; hence anything goes—sexual immorality, whatever."[1]

Modern antinomian Gnostics place a low level of significance on the material body. Their approach is that "only the heart matters," which is part of a "grand divorce" that justifies severing personal behavior from absolute standards of divine design, truth, beauty, and morality. Namely, this type of Gnosticism believes that the body and soul are separate, disjointed entities, rather than functioning as a unit. Therefore, whatever happens to one doesn't affect the other. Consequently, the new Gnosticism touts **that man has the freedom to do whatever he wants with his body, without it impacting his spirituality.**

This type of Gnosticism is seen in our idolatrous culture with its values of boundless self-expression. As a result, we are abandoning God's values of self-control, delayed gratification, and the indirect pursuit of pleasure, which is creating a major collision between God's moral truth and the culture's values. Our calling as born-again believers is to thrive within divinely ordained moral boundaries and limits set by God. These limits were a part of creation, and they were very good. As creatures made in God's image, we are stewards of the creation who are bounded by these limits. The wise and merciful commandments God has placed upon us constitute a safeguard of human love and dignity. Adam's Fall into sin (committed in the name of 'freedom') illustrates the first abandonment of these divinely ordained boundaries and limits.[2]

Darwinism taught us that given enough time we will find a scientific explanation for everything (from maternal love, to the Protestant work ethic, to criminal behavior). The net effect in the minds of most was to replace biblical cosmology (God's 'blueprint') with philosophic naturalism. How did this impact the Western mind? The knowledge of God as personal, transcendent, and involved with creation was eclipsed and demoted.[3] Though evangelicals stressed personal faith and piety, they also began to divide God's role—they saw Him as active in redemption but allowed **the unproven assumptions of science to define the creation and the machinations of psychology to define man and his behavior**.

Consequently, we allowed society to shove God into the 'upper story' where He was no longer Definer of our existence, OR, **involved with the daily details of our lives**. And we all accept this as benign as long as we have Jesus 'in our hearts.' But the Fallout is deadly serious—it contributes the disconnect, opening the gate of the soul to let in the alien invader of porn.[4]

When one allows the Bible to describe salvation and pseudo-science to comprehensively describe the creation, it produces a tear in our thinking. Why? Because the salvation-science dichotomy pictures God as having two radically different faces. It says the side of God that dealt with creation was far less personal than the side of God that dealt with salvation. As a consequence, the Jesus of salvation became very other-worldly and sentimental. He was no longer viewed as Sovereign Lord of the cosmos.

In our humanistic society, God's plan of "the proper constraint of creature before [his sovereign] Creator" becomes obscured. Because there is no transcendent meaning remaining, the greatest goal then becomes what's good for me as there's nothing more than me.[5] This radical 'self-ism' opens the soul to lust and sexual immorality. **When man compartmentalizes God's holy truths to the spiritual realm it produces a wide chasm in his experience.** However, biblical cosmology teaches that the body and soul are designed by God to operate as one. The body expresses the desires and loyalties of the soul. The deeds of the body reveal who our master is and just who or what it is that we are serving (Rom. 6:15-22).

How does this divided view of reality manifest itself in the Evangelical church today? Here is the disturbing answer: redemption tends to be viewed as a private, subjective, personal preference without an objective basis. In this sense, salvation exists only in the mind and heart apart from concrete reality. It is seen as less real than the physical elements of the universe. Christianity deteriorates into a religion of faith only and is no longer grounded upon faith in The Truth.[6]

Evangelicalism's accommodation to the modern, or divided view of truth, has pushed redemption further into the cloudy haze of subjective experience. **As a result, many Christians are living with an open 'gash' between objective and subjective truth.** Consequently the majority of professing Christians have lost the cosmological foundation for redemption—they have lost sight of the unbreakable link between the moral structure of the universe and holy living.

Abandoning Cosmology, "I'm a Christian," yet metaphysically lost.

The absolute truth of cosmology is essential in interpreting the universe.[7] "Cosmology" is that branch of philosophy which deals with the origin and structure of the universe. At the heart of biblical cosmology is both the Creator-creature distinction, and the creation of male and female as the image of God. God's relation to the creation is the ordering principle of the universe and of reality.

In the study of biblical cosmology, we learn that the Creator has set forth His 'blueprint' for His creation. His blueprint is not only our moral map, but also our fixed point of reference which provides our understanding of the nature of reality. All of life is ethical and moral BECAUSE the Author of life and the Creator and Ruler of the universe is holy. Currently, a generation is rising which is oblivious to the fact that God is ultimate reality.

As we mentioned earlier, Darwinism has deepened the divided view of reality. In this fragmented view of reality, quantifiable (measurable) things such as time, space, and mass are considered more real than the transcendentals of truth, beauty, love, purpose, morality, dignity, justice, and rationality.[8] We may accurately say that today's divided view of reality, which places the objective as 'down to earth' and the subjective as 'up in the clouds', has a blinding effect upon people. They view reality as larger than God.

Our Creator's self-revelation in the creation is ignored and explained away; thus, they find their God-given view of first principles increasingly obscured (Rom 1:18-20). **Truth, beauty, love, purpose, morality, and justice are placed in a subjective category and are treated as less real than the matter and motion measurable by science.** Biblical cosmology corrects this misconception by teaching us that the creation is made up of both physical order and moral order. In order to tear down this wall between the two (physical and moral order) we must apply biblical truth to all areas of life.

In the present state of affairs, **it is most common for Christians to begin with soteriology (the doctrine of salvation) instead of cosmology (the doctrine of God's design in creation).** As a result, the doctrine of salvation is easily privatized (reduced to something inward, personal, and pietistic). Without the unifying foundation of cosmology, the rising generation hears biblical principles as disassociated bits and pieces of moral truth instead of seeing God's moral blueprint and creation structures as reality grounded in the character of God. Without cosmology, we cannot see God's moral blueprint as the genuine structure of reality—as the 'very furniture of the universe'!

In the present state of affairs, human sexuality is being redefined. It is being taken out of its moral context and removed from the framework of divine design. In the culture war (which is really a spiritual war) **we are seeing sexuality deconstructed, torn from its teleological framework of divine design and goodness.** The world sees this as acceptable because it has placed a partition, or disconnect between the physical and spiritual realm. As sexuality is reinterpreted according to the worldview of popular culture, we are seeing a new definition of freedom joined to it. **Pop culture is pursuing happiness through freedom from design while in the biblical worldview true happiness is through freedom to design (or freedom in God's design).** The present worldview shift which characterizes modern man's rebellion is characterized by defining freedom and happiness as breaking free from divine design. Redemption in Christ restores a man or woman to rejoice in God's cosmological 'blueprint' for all of life. For in that plan alone is true liberty.

The Human Body: a mere 'Vehicle' or the Center of Moral Volition?

A fragmented worldview without a biblical cosmology will ultimately affect the way one views the human body. Author Randy Alcorn has coined a term for the spiritual-physical disconnect life view: "christo-platonism" (a spirit-body dichotomy patterned after Plato's philosophy, but incorporated into Christianity). In his book titled, Heaven, Alcorn notes that a dichotomized view of the spiritual world and material world is prevalent among Americans. He states that among Americans who believe in the resurrection, two thirds believe we won't have bodies after the resurrection (to have bodies that eat and walk in a physical paradise just sounds so unspiritual).[9]

Christo-platonism views the material realm with its experiences, blessings, and human relationships as "God's competitors, rather than as instruments that communicate His love and character."[10] One woman who read Alcorn's book, Heaven, describes her christo-platonism, "Because I believed that my spirit was really all that mattered to God, I didn't let my body matter to me."[11] Unfortunately, too many Christians are buying into the lie that Christ is interested primarily in the spirit, thus the body is viewed as merely inconsequential. It is easy to see how this opens a huge gateway for sexual immorality of all kinds.

The culture's wrong-headed ideas about spirituality (which are closely related to the rise of the new Gnosticism) are contributing to Christians' misunderstanding of the body. The devaluing of the human body among professing Christians is a symptom of christo-platonism, says Alcorn. "From the christo-platonism perspective, our souls merely occupy our bodies like a hermit crab inhabits a seashell. And [once those bodies are sloughed off,] our souls could naturally, even ideally live in a disembodied state."[12] Needless to say, a Christian holding to this view will won't live a spiritually unified life.

The biblical doctrine of the soul-body unity preserves the truth that the human body was created to be the vehicle of human personality. It is biblical to say that the human form was created for an interactive relationship with God. To abandon this unified view of human nature is to jeopardize the nature of true spirituality. The Gnostic view regards spirituality as something wholly inward, but **that is to divorce the use of the body from its role in true spirituality**—that role expressing itself in the vast **dimension of social corporate relational spirituality.**[13]

I appeal to you therefore, brothers, by the mercies of God, to present your bodies as a living sacrifice, holy and acceptable to God, which is your spiritual worship. [2] Do not be conformed to this world, but be transformed by the renewal of your mind, that by testing you may discern what is the will of God, what is good and acceptable and perfect. Romans 12:1-2 ESV

We are to present our bodies as a living sacrifice. The order is to first present your body and **then you will find your place in the Body of Christ.** Life as a living sacrifice immediately translates into the discovery of your contribution to the body in service. It is common in Evangelicalism to "view the human body as merely physical, a mere mechanical device." But that perspective is a "platonic imposition" upon the biblical view of the personality of man.[14] James Herrick is immensely helpful in providing insight into the Gnostic view of the human body:

The Gnostic view of the body and physical existence runs consistently against the grain of the Revealed Word, a spiritual outlook that elevates both. According to the Word, a personal God intentionally created the physical universe, and it was from the beginning essentially good. Human physical existence—our embodiment—is purposeful and meaningful, not a cosmic accident. People have a body . . . that we might have at our disposal the resources that would allow us to be persons in fellowship and cooperation with a personal God.[15]

The epidemic of cyber-porn among Evangelicals is not merely attributable to technical advances which have increased both availability and anonymity. It is this author's premise that the spirit-body dichotomy contributes to the disconnect between faith and practice found in the lives of so many believers. If you live with the spirit-body dichotomy (disconnect), you are much more likely to let down the drawbridge of the heart and allow the stronghold of the soul to be breached by pornography.

The Ethical Symptoms of Disconnect

The epidemic of Evangelicals viewing pornography may be the most telling index, or symptom, of the Gnostic disconnect. Internet pornography is the unexamined "crime scene"—it is a substantial and traceable contributor to countless devastated lives, dysfunctional families, and divorced couples as well as contributing to spousal abuse and child molestation.

Al Mohler, President of Southern Baptist Theological Seminary, has warned that **"the pervasive plague of pornography represents one of the greatest moral challenges faced by the Christian church in the postmodern age."** Says Mohler, "Eroticism has been woven into the very heart of the culture." And, concerning its breadth of impact upon our culture and our perceptions, he says, "It is virtually impossible to escape the pervasive influence of pornography because it has been mainstreamed through commercial images and entertainment."[16]

"The effects of the sin of pornography extend to almost every area of a person's life," **Mohler continues. "Instead of pointing the sex drive to covenant fidelity in marriage**, it degrades that drive into a sinful passion that robs God of His glory." By yanking God's gift of sexual intimacy from its context of marriage covenant **it is changed into something idolatrous**.[17] The world sees this as permissible because the body and soul are separate. The world's defense is "My spirit and soul are for religion but my body is for myself."

Mohler also states that "pornography represents one of the most insidious attacks upon the sanctity of marriage and the goodness of sex within the one-flesh relationship. **It is the celebration of debauchery rather than purity, and it leads to incalculable harm because it subverts marriage and the marriage bond."**[18] By removing sexual relations from their place in Christian worldview, pornography declares war on God's great purpose of glorifying Himself through the marriage bond. Mohler rightly notes:

[For] marriage is not merely the [lawful] arena of sexual activity, it is presented in Scripture as the divinely-designed arena for the display of God's glory on earth as a man and a wife come together in a one-flesh relationship within the marriage covenant. Rightly understood and rightly ordered, marriage is a picture of God's covenant faithfulness. Marriage is to display God's glory, reveal God's good gifts to His creatures, and protect human beings from the inevitable disaster that follows when sexual passions are divorced from their rightful place.[19]

However, the Gnostic disconnect 'guts' or rips out the transcendental aspect from sexual relations. As Mohler observed, the world is using sex to fulfill its own selfish desires. The Gnostic disconnect is telling the world that every sexual expression is okay because sexuality is a separate entity from the spiritual realm. As a result, the Gnostic disconnect paves the way for people to commit all types of sexual immorality because the spirit, body, and soul are not one.

Mohler argues that by divine design God's gift of sexuality is meant to pull us out of ourselves and our self-occupied concerns and desires and toward our spouse. A husband cannot have a secret 'disconnected' life of pursuing lust and then expect to have God-glorifying emotional and sexual intimacy with his wife. **The man committed to sexual purity is living in a state of sexual integrity toward his wife.** In order to pursue their mutual pleasure in the marriage bed, the husband "is careful to live, to talk, to lead, and to love in such a way that **his wife finds her fulfillment in giving herself to him in love."** Their marital relations then become "the fulfillment of the entire relationship, and not an isolated physical act that is merely self-centered personal pleasure." "[T]his man can be confident that he is fulfilling his responsibilities both as a male and as a man. . . His sexual desires are being directed toward the one-flesh relationship that is the perfect paradigm of God's intention in creation."[20] This is, by God's plan, the polar opposite of disconnect.

Sexual relations in marriage as a holistic expression are significant for how we are to understand the unity of God's plan for husband and wife. Marital relations, as God designed them, are character-building and culture-making. These relations are character-building because a man brings his entire lifestyle of masculine responsibility to the marriage bed. And, marital relations are culture-making because emotional and spiritual bonding takes place. These bonds are essential to the building up of the family environment in which children are nurtured and instructed so as to develop the ability to shape culture.[21] A man's role in character-building and culture-making demand that he operates from the position of soul-body unity and not from the lie of soul-body disconnect.

Now, by way of radical contrast, consider another man enmeshed in the disconnect who uses his sex drive as a dynamo of lust. As he turns to pornography, his desires are

NOT turned toward a spouse; but are turned inward. His arousal through illicit images is tantamount to the seduction of the imagination **and the corruption of his soul.**[22] This self-directed misuse of sexual desire becomes a 'tutorial' in selfishness. We are warned in 2 Peter 2:14 that by habitually sowing to lust it is possible to develop "a heart trained in greed." Mohler chides his disobedient readers with the following admonition:

Pornography is a slander against the goodness of God's creation and a corruption of this good gift God has given His creatures out of His own self-giving love. To abuse this gift is to weaken, not only the institution of marriage, but the fabric of civilization itself. To choose lust over love is to debase humanity and to worship the false god Priapus in the most brazen form of idolatry. The deliberate use of pornography is nothing less than the willful invitation of illicit lovers and objectified sex objects. . . **The damage to a man's heart is beyond measure, and the cost in human misery will only be made clear on the Day of Judgment**. . . In this society, we are called to be nothing less than a corps of the mutually accountable amidst a world that lives as if it will never be accountable.[23]

Like an unseen internal parasite, porn feeds upon the very faculties of soul which we need for kindness, gentleness, self-control, empathy, mercy, and agape love. In Kevin Scott's book, "The Porning of America," the author observes that "the influence of porn on mainstream culture is affecting our self perceptions and behavior in everything from fashion to body image to how we conceptualize our sexuality. Our kids are growing up in a "hyper-sexualized" environment. In MySpace photos and cell phone 'sexting' teens are imitating the porn they have actually seen and absorbed through the internet.[24]

"Internet porn plays a part in an increasing number of divorce cases," notes author Ross Douthat, who has gleaned this fact from a survey of matrimonial lawyers. This has prompted Douthat to pose the question, "Is pornography use a form of adultery [for a married man]?" He "suggests that we should . . . **regard infidelity as a continuum of betrayal.**" In other words,

"The internet era has ratcheted the experience of pornography much closer to adultery than I suspect most porn users would like to admit."[25] It is high time we warn our Christian brothers that porn use in any amount deepens the lying deception that the body is disconnected from the spirit. The satanic lie has always been that the deeds of the body are inconsequential to one's spiritual state. In the Garden of Eden it was, 'you may eat and not risk death and damnation'. Today the ancient Lie is propelling us toward Armageddon at warp speed.

A widening Disconnect broadened by Techno-Consumer Culture

Author and professor of literature and film studies, Grant Horner opines that "the [computer] screen has been framed as the real world—we have gone from Windows as a 'window' to the world—to Windows is the world. The screen has become the world." The screen is moving ever closer to the brain. The fighter pilot of previous wars looked out of his windscreen at the enemy. Now the computer display is often on the canopy of the cockpit and the latest technology offers the pilot another display on special contact lenses.

All this to say that the screen "presents a limited visual space that [increasingly stands for] our entire visual plane. . . The screen is more than a window on the world—the screen is the world, as it is."[26] Life in front of a computer screen has plunged us into "a far more 'immersive' state of consciousness than working in a factory or on a farm," says Horner. "The screen has become THE visual space, visuality itself."[27]

The "pornification of culture" is shaping the way in which this society approaches sexual curiosity and the way in which it invents itself sexually. The vision of freedom without truth has radically removed the body from the realm of the sacred. Philosopher Michel championed this disastrous view of human freedom. His false view of personal liberty sends the message of no consequence sex. The result is a generation immersed in erotica and with mangled lives to show for it.[28] Auto-eroticism in front of a computer screen is sucking the life out of professing Christian men. The sexual compromise of internet porn makes a man 'mute' for Christ. It 'hollows out' his godly masculinity and makes his sword of truth inactive, corroding it to its scabbard where it sits useless, immobile, and idle.

Sexual Sin—misplaced Drive or Dysfunctional Worship?

When sex is taken out of its good, God-given context, it becomes a false integration point which fragments the person. Sex in its proper context, as said earlier, is a God-honoring celebration of our respective masculinity and femininity in covenant. We see this glorious truth best when we realize that the body and spirit are created by God to function as one. Marital relations are meant by God to deepen a man's character and godly masculinity—and there is very clear reason for this.

The marriage bed is to be the consummation and expression of a man's whole life of godly masculinity toward his wife. In that sense, marital relations are unifying for the married couple. When we bow before God's good, wise, and just creation structures, it strengthens and enhances our humanity because we are functioning according to our design and according to the goal of divine teleology. In other words, the man is living for God's honor by living as His image.

By contrast, viewing illicit pornographic images fragments a man and leaves him with sexual brokenness. In essence, pornography is a kind of theft—it involves taking what is not ours. It short circuits character-building by allowing a man to serve the idol of pleasure and to experience a rush of endorphins. There is a momentary pleasure payoff, but **without the character-building price of service, leadership, communication, love, and self-denial.** Direct self-focused self-gratification brings the Fallout of personal shame. It corrupts the soul because it enslaves and degrades, debasing a man to operate on the level of animal passions. God in Christ has an infinitely better plan for us.

End Chapter Questions:

1. Why does the use of internet porn deepen a person's selfishness and decrease their ability to love God and others?
2. When we think of doing certain things habitually, or as a practice, how would practicing holiness train us in righteousness? How would porn use train a person in greed and selfishness?
3. Will we be simply spirits in heaven, or will we have bodies that can interact with others and the creation?

Endnotes:

[1] Tim Gallant, "Material Girls and Boys," (www.truth-and-beauty.com) p. 1

[2] Ibid.

[3] Ibid.

[4] Ibid.

[5] James White, *Alpha Omega Ministries,* 11/5/08 webcast

[6] Vishal Mangalwadi, "How Christianity lost America," 2011

[7] Dave Doveton.

[8] Divinely ordained *teleology* (or design), is the foundation of these transcendentals.

[9] Randy Alcorn, *Heaven* (Tyndale, 2004), pp. 52, 112

[10] Ibid, p. 176

[11] Ibid, p. 481

[12] Alcorn, p. 112

[13] Dallas Willard, *The Spirit of the Disciplines* (Harper and Row, San Francisco, CA, 1988) p. 77

[14] Ibid, p. 82

[15] James Herrick, *The Making of the New Spirituality* (InterVarsity Press, Downers Grove, IL, 2003) p. 271

[16] Al Mohler, "The Seduction of Pornography," *Boundless Webzine.* 2005, p. 1

[17] Ibid.

[18] Ibid., p. 2

[19] Ibid.

[20] Ibid.

[21] Interview with Vishal Mangalwadi, missionary to India

[22] Ibid, p. 3

[23] Ibid, pp. 3-4

[24] Kevin Scott in "The Pornification of a Generation," book review, Jessica Bennett, *Newsweek,* 10/7/08

[25] Ross Douthat in Roberto Rivera y Carlo, "Porn Adultery & Marriage" *Boundless Webzine,* 2005

[26] Grant Horner, "Theorizing the Weightless Rhetoric of the Digital Spatialization of Knowledge," (The Master's College, Santa Clarita, CA, 2007), p. 5

[27] Ibid, p. 8

[28] Ravi Zacharias, "An Ancient Message, through Modern Means, to a Postmodern Mind," Jon Hinkson and Greg Ganssle, "Epistemology at the Core of Postmodernism: Rorty, Foucault, and the Gospel," *Telling the Truth,* D. A. Carson, Gen. Ed. (Zondervan, Grand Rapids, MI, 2000), pp. 24, 83

Section 9

The Gnostic Disconnect Part 2

Section Objectives

1. To understand that when we feed on God's glorious vision for male and female, the lustful counterfeit offered by the world loses its appeal.

2. To learn that consecration to God involves presenting our bodies as a living sacrifice to God; which is our 'reasonable service of worship'.

3. To understand that joyful freedom takes place when we bring every area of our lives under the lordship of Christ.

4. To recognize that the devil's 'cosmology' contains the lie that we may rip God's gifts from the divine blueprint and not experience consequences.

A Biblical Strategy for solving the Disconnect

How do we solve the *disconnect* which so readily allows for the entrance of sexual sin—how do we get faith and life 'reconnected' again? *Sexual sin is actually a dysfunction in worship. Sexual idolatry is the activity of seeking fulfillment and integration (wholeness) by means of a substitute god.* Greg Johnson, author of *The World According to God*, states that "sexual healing requires that we be trained again in the proper worship of God. A heart trained in delight in God finds the promises of sin unimpressive."[1]

God has a glorious "greater vision" for sexual relations. "When we give sex the greater vision God has for it, its sinful imitation [pornography] loses its luster" (John Piper). This is foundational to the healing of sexual brokenness and sexual addiction. There is healing in Christ for sexually shattered lives, and that healing involves praise and affirmation for God's design of male and female in a marriage covenant of spiritual oneness.

Believers trapped in patterns of sexual lust need a biblical strategy that is holistic. This proactive strategy for victory must include: retraining in worship, rebuilding the biblical view of sexuality, and reclaiming the truth that our body is a chief spiritual resource. In his book, The God of Sex, Peter Jones has established clearly that pornography **deconstructs**, or fractures God's design for sexuality. Therefore, any ministry dedicated to freeing believers from sexual brokenness must reconstruct sexuality biblically.[2]

A weak grasp of God's vision for male and female is symptomatic of the fact that contemporary Christianity is starving for cosmology—for the wonder of God's glorious 'blueprint' for marital oneness. As evidence of the absence of cosmology, too many professing believers have attempted to "add God to their lives." In a narcissistic fashion they have asked, "Where does God fit into my life?" They should be asking the cosmological questions, "Where does my life fit into this great story of God's mission?" And, "What is man's ultimate purpose and place in the cosmos?" The Bible is "the real story of reality to which we are called to conform ourselves."[3] That biblical vision for life has the power to blast us out of our false dichotomies (disconnects). Christians need to hear the full biblical truth concerning what a spiritual resource their bodies are.

Is the Human Body a fleshly 'Beast of Burden' or a Spiritual Resource?

When we use our bodies for the spiritual ends for which we were saved, we are cooperating with **the Holy Spirit's goal or conformity to Christ.** When I consecrate myself to God, I must be aware that surrender of self is inseparable from giving up my body to Him in such a way that it can serve both Him and me as a common abode, as John 14:23, 1 Corinthians 6:15-20, and Ephesians 2:22 testify."[4]

Because it is so common for believers to contemplate salvation apart from creation (biblical cosmology), it is also common for believers to buy into an 'other worldly' brand of spirituality that is **inward, private, and compartmentalized**. This is one of the key factors in producing the *disconnect* between body and spirit in the mind of a believer. When the doctrine of salvation is NOT anchored in cosmology, it opens the door to esoteric (inward only) spirituality with its mind-body dichotomy. Central to the "cure" for the *disconnect* (with its faulty view of spirituality and the body) is a hearty willingness to embrace God's great blueprint and comprehensive plan for our whole existence.

Scripture calls believers to regard their bodies as a great spiritual resource. The divine purpose of the human body is central to biblical worldview. Scripture tells us that "the body is for the Lord," and that **through the reality of organic living union with Christ, we are "members of Christ"** (1 Cor. 6:13, 15). By living according to this perspective, we guard against the notion that the "spiritual is something wholly inward, or just kept between the individual and God."[6]

To view the body as a spiritual resource is to live the Christian life holistically. That mindset is in touch with the reality that true spirituality involves a huge corporate, social dimension in which one's body is used in Christian fellowship. The body is made available to Christ as we exercise our spiritual gifts while others are edified and served in the process.[7]

This is of course the outcome of offering one's body back to God as a "living sacrifice" (Rom. 12:1-2). The context of Romans 12 is the building up of the corporate body of Christ and doing so *through* the sacrificial service of the individual members of the body. The result is not acceleration in private piety, but a lifestyle of consecration to God characterized by interrelatedness with other believers. It is by means of the dedication of our bodies that we enjoy fulfilling our part in the life of the corporate body.

When we employ that mentality, we are cognizant that our gifts function in a complementary manner. We collectively make up the body of Christ, and we live to edify the members of the body of Christ in all of our relationships (12:4-6ff.).

The Body is the Battlefield of Worldview

Our rising generation has been so indoctrinated with disconnect ideology that we need constant reminders that the body is the battlefield of worldview. The Apostle Paul uses language to evoke powerful imagery in Romans 6:13—he calls the members of our bodies "weapons" to be used for righteousness. So paramount is the concept of the body as an instrument of righteousness that the principle of presentation (to righteousness or to unrighteousness) is cast as an "either-or" proposition. Believers are to yield, or present, the members of their bodies to God and not to unrighteousness.

If Christians do not regard their bodies to be a resource of spiritual life as God intends, then they will tend to despise or disregard the spiritual significance of their bodies.[8] A "de-sacralization" of the body will be a natural consequence of denying the spiritual importance of the human body. This denial involves dismissing the fact that the body is sacred—the temple of the Holy Spirit (1 Corinthians 6:19).

By "desacralize" we mean to discount the role of the body in our "spiritual service of worship" (Rom 12:1). **Desacralization** of the body often means that the believer regards his or her body to be **a hindrance to true spirituality**, rather than **a pivotal resource to true spirituality.**

The spirit-body dichotomy inherent in the "Gnostic impulse" stands in stark contrast to Paul's reasoning. Paul regarded his personal holiness to be joined to the exertion of effort to bring **his body in subjection to God's will** (1 Cor 9:23-27). The Apostle made it his ambition to be pleasing to the Lord that he might stand before Christ and have a favorable judgment in regards to the deeds done in his body (2 Cor. 5:9-10ff.).

Paul constantly affirmed that the body was *for the Lord*, and the Lord is for the body (1 Cor. 6:13). In our consecration to God, we are to be conscious of the fact that the members of our physical body are to be considered **instruments, or 'weapons' of righteousness** (Rom. 6:13). Though the Apostle's desire was to receive his glorified body at the coming of Christ (2 Cor. 5:4-8), he regarded the believer's earthly existence to be bound up in presenting one's body to God as a living sacrifice. For Paul this was not exceptional, but essential to "our reasonable service of worship" (Rom. 12:1-2).

God's Truths unite our Christian Experience

We need to recapture the necessity and priority of transformation by God's truth. Many, if not all of us, have received **salvation truths** 'devotionally'—that is, **disconnected from cosmology**, disconnected from God's plan for the creation, and disconnected from divine transcendence. As a consequence of marginalizing these truths, these principles do not exercise the necessary force and influence to order, animate, and constrain their lives.[9] Is it any wonder that those within our Christian sphere so often greet Christian precepts with apathy?

Without the doctrine of transcendence, **salvation truths are thrust into an upper story subjective category,** divorced from the divine blueprint found in biblical cosmology. A disconnect follows which is characterized by distancing spiritual truth from the everyday decisions of life. **An open gash develops between faith and life.** One of the most common ways Christian people respond to this disconnect is by **seeking an identity based upon the development of self through the consumption of goods and services, through amusement, and through personal preferences,** rather than upon the Creator's story. What also suffers due to this disconnect is the proper perception of our bodies—we tend NOT to regard our bodies as a spiritual resource. Thus, we reiterate, that it is precisely at this juncture that pornography may find an unguarded entry point into the believer's life.

Removing the Disconnect by reuniting Reality in Christ

Christ does what Plato and the Greek philosophers could not do, He unifies all reality. **He links visible and invisible reality and He reconciles singularity and plurality.** He gives harmony, unity, and order to the cosmos. The Son connects all of the realms of *being* (permanence) and *becoming* (change)." This is intensely significant that Christ unifies all reality in Himself—temporal and eternal, physical and non-physical. According to Colossians 1:15-20, it is the Father's purpose that Christ have "first place" in every realm; visible and invisible. There is no dichotomy, no disconnect in the divine order of things.

As Christians, we locate truth in the Person of Jesus Christ—"all of the treasures of wisdom and knowledge are in Him" (Col 2:3). The great implication drawn from His lordship over all knowledge is that what He promises and threatens are immutable.[10] He will make good on His promises and His threats. Therefore, "for the Christian, truth has the character and element of trust."[11] This is highly important in our postmodern culture of distrust which tends to throw reliance back upon self. By contrast, the true believer rejoices in his dependence upon Christ. For our

Lord is preeminent and supreme; He has first place in all things (Col 1:18). He fills all in all (Eph 1:23; 4:10).

In light of the vastness and dignity of Christ's Person, it is immensely significant that the Scriptures promise us as believers that we are complete in Him (Col 2:10). Our wholeness and completeness is built around the Person of Christ. By means of the infinite value of His substitutionary death, He has 'purchased us' to be His possession—we no longer belong to ourselves (1 Cor 6:19-20; Titus 2:14). Therefore, our devotion to our sovereign Lord Jesus is inseparable from the fact that our body is to be at His disposal, consecrated to Him for worship and service as the very 'temple of His Spirit' (1 Cor 6:18-20). Do you see how this eliminated the *disconnect* in our lives?

Right thinking is the key. As new creatures, believers are to jettison the old perspective of fragmented worldview and carnal thinking. Paul commands the Corinthians to regard no one from the perspective of the old worldview anymore (2 Cor. 5:16). "The goal of Christian worldview is not private [piety], but as Christ promised, the goal is toward a peaceful and just society."[12] T. Austin Sparks captures the 'incarnational' dimension of believers living together in love and truth by stating "that God is never satisfied with anything less than the fullness of His Son as represented by His Church."[13]

It is all too common for believers to see obedience as a narrow bandwidth and not whole life affections. The assumptions of popular culture only deepen this misconception that life may be successfully divided up by means of a sacred-secular split. God's claims upon us in Christ blast into our false sacred-secular dichotomy and tell us that the Lord claims every square foot of our life experience for Himself. Biblical worldview blasts us out of dualistic thinking. Christian integration (a unified Christian life experience) is provided by Christ and His incarnation; for He came as the Great Physician to make us whole.

"The incarnation [of Jesus Christ] does not let us partition reality into spiritual and non-spiritual spheres—but

shows us that all reality flows from one integrative source." Christians are to develop a holistic worldview by "critical reflection on life in light of the incarnation of Christ."[14]

Without God's view of the world, the popular culture will assume the default role of setting our worldview agenda. The answer is to study and proclaim the full-orbed gospel of Christ—who is both Creator and Redeemer. Believers are to live so as to bring every area of life under the Lordship of Christ. Only then will they be able to abandon all disconnects and enjoy a unified Christian experience. John Piper's exhortation which joins Christ's supremacy to our unified worldview is also very valuable:

Christ is like the sun in our solar system. In this analogy, planets represent the goals, desires, and responsibilities of the believer. Christ's majesty is like the blazing glory and gravitational pull of the sun—the orbits of the planets are held and guided by His preeminence. When Christ is central in our lives; the 'planets' of our desires and goals and labors are ordered by Christ and put into their proper orbits.

When we are captivated by the supremacy of Christ and ravished by all that God is toward us in Christ and all that He has promised to be toward us in Christ, then our hearts are enlarged to take in more of our Lord. *The more that happens, the more the soul is broadened to take in the majesty of our God. As we grow in that direction, God is big; and lusts are small—sexuality, with its 'little' thrill, assumes its proper size and orbit in our life; sexual lust loses its power over us.*

The solution to this pervasive problem [of the 'small soul'] is drawn from our created purpose; the human soul was created to find unending satisfaction in Christ, for in Christ God gives us Himself. Only the supremacy of Christ is big enough to enlarge the soul [majestic landscapes such as the Grand Canyon, the Himalayas, the Milky Way Galaxy can inspire, but not expand the soul.]

Our problem today is that churches are full of folks with little souls. The evil one knows this; he is opportunistic; he is using the world to send tsunami waves through the back door of the church—we're awash in lust and sexual addiction. There is a clear reason for this. If we were created for soul-staggering grandeur; and our hearts and minds are disconnected from that majesty that is the supremacy of Christ; then it is not surprising that hearts have settled onto trivial things. The human heart was made to be lost in wonder, love, awe, and praise—if the heart is not staggered by the supremacy of Christ, then it will tend to reach for the greatest natural high it can get—sex.

The deepest cure for sexual lust is to be emotionally staggered by the supremacy of Christ. The sheer weight of Christ and eternity constitutes the gravity of what life is all about. So massive and heavy is that weight, that to have felt the tiniest portion of it makes it almost emotionally impossible to go to the internet to view porn.[15]

Biblical cosmology is our lens for viewing ultimate reality. When we analyze life by means of the authoritative perspective of biblical cosmology, there is an intensely satisfying intellectual worshipful fulfillment in seeing the unity of all knowledge and the wisdom of divine purposes.

The use of pornography involves a kind of alienation and disconnect from the unifying power of biblical cosmology. This is because porn stresses an anatomical ideal of the human body that is completely divorced from *transcendentals* (transcendentals are defined as God's truth, beauty, categories, relationships, moral order, glory, righteousness, goodness, and justice). Transcendentals are inseparable from a blueprint for our lives that is joined to God's glory. Thus, they provide the moral context for all of God's good gifts to us, His creatures.

That means that when God's good gifts are ripped and torn from their moral context of divine transcendentals, the result is idolatry. The beautiful gift of sexual oneness in marriage, if allowed to run in the gutter like waste water, becomes smut. God is dishonored when we tear His good gifts from their moral context. As Christian men, we need to instruct ourselves and our brothers in the truth that a divided life is a life of hypocrisy. Porn is a worldview of *disconnect* (between soul and body)—and viewing it only deepens the Gnostic disconnect.

As men we are very vulnerable to the desire to seek sexual erotic intimacy outside of the marriage covenant. It is a driving force within our natures which is why pornography is such a temptation. The use of porn involves the isolation of erotic pleasure from its divinely ordained context of transcendentals.

This is of course why porn is ultimately unsatisfying— like a thirsty man who attempts to slake his parched throat with seawater, destruction of his life and health are the result. Delving into illicit images is like reaching out to touch a mirage. What appears to be there in the shimmering desert image is but an illusion. The mirage's promises of cool water are deceptive.

Porn promises but can't deliver because it unravels the parts of God's gift that are designed to remain joined (sexuality, love, covenant, and spirituality). Therefore to bring the yearning of our natures to porn is like attempting to drink from a sun-scorched sand dune. This ripping apart of sexual pleasure from the marriage bond may deliver moments of excitement, but those moments are immediately followed by a descent into shame and self disgust. The ongoing Fallout of shame just keeps dragging a man deeper into cynicism and uncaring attitudes. The porn user ends up lower than when he started because he has thrown away divine cosmology and related to God's creation in an idolatrous fashion. It is no exaggeration to say that the porn user is buying into someone else's cosmology (i.e. Lucifer's).

Porn use says in effect, "I accept the devil's cosmology." The devil's initial temptation was a solicitation to believe that beauty can safely and happily exist when removed from its divine moral context. Porn deconstructs creational structures. And biblical theism is eroded in the process. Cosmology and biblical theism belong together—you can't have one completely intact without the other.   Porn wages war on biblical cosmology (which is ultimately fighting against God

Himself who ordained and ordered this moral universe and its creation structures).

Closely associated with our view of the human body is our philosophy of beauty. Biblical cosmology states that beauty has no existence independent from the Creator. Beauty has always been joined to divinely ordained transcendentals. Beauty in its divinely ordained moral context of truth gives glory to God. Aesthetics therefore (in their cosmological context of creation structure) are pointers to the glory of God. We love this beauty for the sake of God's glory, and not for the sake of our own desires alone, or for the sake of the excellence of the created thing itself.

Of course this is why beauty is the battleground for the souls of men and women. As it was in the beginning with the lie in Eden, beauty was the battlefield. Satan traps, enslaves, dupes, and leads into idolatry by removing beauty from the very transcendentals necessary for beauty to point to the glory of God. The deceiver infers that beauty can stand alone and be indulged in by itself. The gospel delivers from this lie by placing us in Christ and causing us to discern all things from the perspective of the mind of Christ (1 Cor. 2:12-16). Therefore, the very depth of what we love as maturing believers must hinge upon finding excellence in created things for Christ's sake.

Biblical cosmology is a unifying principle. When properly understood it eliminates the compartments we have constructed in our lives. Biblical cosmology imbues upon us that every square inch of our experience belongs to God—there are no compartments, no partitions. As this truth pervades our lives it will allow body and soul to operate as the unity God intends.

Pornography is sexual idolatry because it gives the honor due to God to created things. Postmodern culture with its pervasive relativism has exacerbated the problem by blinding us to the immensity and eternality of God's moral government. As denizens of postmodern culture we are often insulated from the immovable ineffable strictness of moral cause and effect. We are frequently oblivious to the inescapable principle of sowing and reaping (Rom. 2:5-9). But God is 'not mocked'—harvest day is coming—men will reap what they have sown (Gal. 6:7).

Modern sinners downplay the seriousness of their sin by affirming that their infractions do not hurt others. They even say that sexual immorality doesn't harm their body or anyone else's. It seems they have forgotten that the first tablet of God's holy law is meant to safeguard love and honor to God. All sin, whether a violation of the first of second tablet, **is against God Himself** (Ps 51:4). Because our created identity is that of a worshipper, all sin is a failure to value God as He deserves. In our age of license people seem oblivious to what they owe God. As a consequence, they normalize their idolatry (Col 3:5).

Idolatry defaces the image of God in man and fragments the human unity of soul and body by making the body the instrument of sin. Lucifer's express purpose is to use idolatry as the means of working against God's purpose of making man and woman in His image and likeness. The evil one cannot change our ontology (creational identity) or human make up directly, but he can do it indirectly. His tool of choice is idolatry. Idol worship in all its forms defaces and fragments the image of God in us. The enemy used the ancient lie to sever us from the knowledge of God and to attach us to the world as our 'preferred source of fulfillment.' Satan's hatred of God is expressed in his malevolent wish to shatter the image of God in us by means of idolatry. The evil one uses lust to make us listless and apathetic about staying free through holiness—he wants us to drop our diligence and to devalue our liberty in the Lord.

The evil one knows we are created to be worshippers. And he knows that the worship of God is our freedom, and the worship of idols is servitude. Therefore, idolatry is inseparable from de-humanizing bondage. When we take the glory, attention, adoration, and devotion that belongs to God and give it to created things, we are committing idolatry. Bondage and servitude is the enduring consequence.

Porn, or sexual idolatry, is a dysfunction in worship. Idolatry weakens the very things that true worship is

designed to strengthen; our freedom and liberty in Christ, the unity of our Christian experience, our humanness, and our ability to reflect God's character as the image of God. The remedy for our brokenness is Christ Himself. The gospel promises us that in Him we are complete (Col. 2:10). This means that our former fragmentation by sin is 'healed' in Christ. Now we are to live out our completeness in Christ by presenting members of our body to God daily (Rom. 6:11-13). The Apostle Paul tells us in that the members of our body are like strategic 'weapons' which carry out the agenda or campaign of our master. Obedience is therefore a 'whole soul and body endeavor'. Again, this is how we can eliminate the disconnect.

Biblical cosmology is God's blueprint for us, the very opposite of the disconnect we see in our culture. To the degree that our lives are ordered according to His 'blueprint' is the degree to which we are in touch with reality. Evangelicalism is 'doctrinally emaciated' without biblical cosmology. For those who have lived self-directed lives, despising the divine blueprint, reality will hit like a thousand sledge hammers on the day of judgment. They will discover to their horror that their sinful self-direction did not create a new reality. This is God's world—it operates in the precise ways He has determined. This knowledge is central to the fear of God—it is His universe.

The relation of man to woman was the first 'boundary' and design that the Lord formalized with the institution of marriage. God established, then blessed, then formalized by matrimony the creational design of one man designed for one woman for life (Gen. 2:18-25). This *creation structure* involves the participation of our body and soul in the marriage relationship (1 Cor. 6:15-20). The cosmological (creational) structures established by God are filled with His goodness, justice, and wisdom. As mentioned, these constitute a 'blueprint' for us by which we are to be governed. Only by our alignment with this blueprint can we truly say that we are walking with God—serving Him, obeying Him, demonstrating loyalty to Him. The rejection of this divinely ordained 'blueprint' is the dishonoring of God. This is why porn is such a serious sin—it is a declaration of war upon God's goodness reflected in His all-wise 'blueprint' for us.

Christian husbands and fathers need to be protectors against the disconnect that severs the roles of soul and body. As Christian men, we need to blast sexual lust out of the small truncated category in which we have placed it. It is all too often relegated to the 'little' zone called "my problem with sexual lust." Biblical cosmology helps us burst the issue of mortification of sexual sin out of too small a category in which we have treated it as "just my private bosom sin and personal heart struggle." No, cosmology smashes through this artificial disconnect and shrunken perspective by bringing us face to face with God's infinite wisdom in founding reality upon His all-wise and just creational structures.

Man's humanness and dignity are inseparable from the fact that as the image of God, he is a 'bounded' creature. The limits, or boundaries which God has placed upon us are at the heart of our creaturehood and our humanness. As the only order of creatures made in the divine image, we must find our purpose in our creational identity—that identity being to reflect the moral majesty of our Creator with our whole being, both soul and body. Our problem as men (locked in combat with sexual lust) is that we have tended to see God's commands against impurity as separated from God's plan.

As a consequence, we all too often resemble the world's mindset when we imagine (even for a moment) that God's laws against sexual impurity are but a religious imposition of morality upon society as opposed to being the moral fabric of the universe and reality itself. This is why we must hear biblical truth through the perspective of biblical worldview. Only then will we have the totalizing picture that puts the universe together (Rom. 11:33-36).

We desperately need our worldview strengthened so that we understand the seriousness of the implications of allowing the disconnect to open us to the worship of created things. Your body is the temple of the Holy Spirit. That means that we function as His hands, feet, and voice—expressing the personality of Christ through the activity of our bodies. Your body is your chief spiritual resource. No wonder the Apostle Paul says to the Corinthians (many of which were trapped in the Gnostic disconnect), "the body is not for immorality, but for the Lord; and the Lord is for the body" (1 Cor. 6:13). The Gnostic disconnect (and its accompanying immorality) is not private sin—it affects the health of the entire body of Christ. This disobedience is a serious matter.

We are commanded to daily commit our body-soul unity to the Lord as His possession. The biblical call to offer ourselves (body and soul) to the Lord as a living sacrifice has an immediate corporate application (Rom. 12:1-2). In this passage of offering ourselves to God, Paul uses the word "body" to refer to the whole self—the whole human life.[16] When we yield our whole being to the Lord as a 'living sacrifice," we are placing our bodies at His disposal in order to be a blessing to the members of Christ's Body. "For just as we have many members in one body and all the members do not have the same function, so we who are many, are one body in Christ, and individually members one of another" (Rom. 12:4-5).

The human being as the image of God also requires body-soul unity. As a new creation in Christ the dichotomy of soul and body is removed. We realize God has made both to be united in worship and service to Him. Our body and soul working together reflects the very character of our Maker. Being possessed by God does not mean only our spiritual life is His but our bodies as well. Christ died to make us whole—to ultimately remove every vestige of disconnect. Why go back to the disconnect He died to remove? The cross of Christ joins faith and life by 'crucifying' the idolatrous divide that allows for compartmentalized religion.

Endnotes:

[1] Greg Johnson, *The World according to God* (InterVarsity Press, Downers Grove, IL, 2002) pp. 141-142

[2] Peter Jones, *The God of Sex* (Victor Books, Cook Communications, Colorado Springs, CO, 2006) pp. 21-26

[3] Christopher J. H. Wright, *The Mission of God* (InterVarsity Press Academic, Downers Grove, IL, 2006), pp. 533-534

[4] Dallas Willard, *The Spirit of the Disciplines* (Harper & Row Publishers, San Francisco, CA, 1988), pp. 30-31

[5] Greg Johnson, p. 21

[6] Dallas Willard, pp. 76-77

[7] Ibid.

[8] Ibid, pp. 89-90

[9] Ibid, pp. 125, 128

[10] By "epistemic lordship" is meant that Christ, as lord of all knowledge, is the final source, authority, and arbiter of truth—He is our epistemology—our basis for knowing what we know with absolute certainty.

[11] Norman Klassen and Jens Zimmerman, *The Passionate Intellect* (Baker Publishing), pp. 30-31

[12] Ibid, p. 151

[13] T. Austin Sparks, *The Prophetic Ministry,* p. 22

[14] Ibid, pp. 186-187, 195

[15] John Piper, *Sex and the Supremacy of Christ,* Conference, Bethlehem Baptist Church, Minneapolis, MN

[16] Ranald Macauly and Jerram Barrs, *Being Human: The Nature of Spiritual Experience* (InterVarsity Press: Downers Grove, Illinois, 1978), p. 53.

THE MISSION FOR GOSPEL FOR LIFE

Jay Wegter
College Professor,
Speaker, Writer
Executive Director,
Gospel for Life

His passion to help the church recover her New Testament mission, Jay founded *Gospel for Life* in 2005. *GFL* is a training ministry which assists local churches in fulfilling The Great Commission through evangelistic outreach and through curriculum designed to keep the Gospel central in discipleship. *GFL* provides equipping in leadership development, evangelism, apologetics and discipleship, and in grace-driven sanctification (www.gospelforlife.org). Jay's week is typically occupied with men's ministry, worldview mentoring and discipleship. He is a traveling speaker, providing workshops on Men's Ministry; Evangelism and Discipleship Training; and Christian Worldview. He regularly presents his course on Worldview Evangelism at churches and Bible institutes. Jay is also a professional artist. His work can be viewed online at www.jaywegter.com.

Jay is co-author of the book, "This Little Church had None," published by Evangelical Press of England. This book was the featured gift book at the Shepherds' Conference in 2009. Jay has also written resources on the Christian life. Titles include the following: "30 Days of Transforming Grace," "Christ's Pattern for His Church: Disciples making Disciples," "The Purity Workbook for Men," and "How to Share the Gospel in a Post-Christian World."